A TREE
IN YOUR
POCKET

JACQUELINE MEMORY PATERSON

D0999090

Thorsons
An Imprint of HarperCollinsPublishers

Thorsons
An Imprint of HarperCollins*Publishers*
77–85 Fulham Palace Road,
Hammersmith, London W6 8JB

Published by Thorsons 1998
10 9 8 7 6 5 4

Jacqueline Memory Paterson asserts the moral
right to be identified as the author of this work

A catalogue record for this book
is available from the British Library

ISBN 0 7225 3778 6

Printed in Great Britain by Woolnough Bookbinding Limited,
Irthlingborough, Northamptonshire

CONTENTS

And do you remember what secrets the trees told us as we lay under their shady branches on the hot mid-summer days, while the leaves danced and flickered against the blue, blue sky? Can you tell what was the charm that held us like a dream in the falling dusk, as we watched their heavy masses grow dark against the silvery twilight sky?

C. E. Smith, *Trees*

THE
ENGLISH
YEW

IRISH/GAELIC	*Ioho*
OGHAM	䷜
RUNIC	ᛂ
RULING PLANET	Saturn
ABILITIES	Guardian to the Door of Rebirth. Rest after the struggle of life. Divination. Dowsing. Bows. To do with the element of Earth.
SEASON	Winter
YEW	*Taxus baccata*. Evergreen. POISONOUS.

The yew tree helped form the great primeval conifer forests which dominated the earth long before the advent of broadleaved trees. It lives for over 1,000 years and it is thought that many living yews pre-date Christ by many thousands of years. The Fortingall Yew in Perthshire is claimed to be up to 9,000 years old. Many yews are mentioned in the Domesday Book of 1086 and one of the oldest weapons found is a crude yew spear from the Old Stone Age.

The yew gains its capacity for great age from its particular growth of shoots or branches, which root into the ground and grow to form new trunks. These then join the main trunk and become part of it, which gives yews huge fluted girths. It takes 150 years for the main trunk to form and then the yew continues its growth widthways. In old age it continues to grow, even with a completely hollow trunk. This has given yew a reputation for immortality and has made it a symbol of life after death. The yew is common in churchyards and in undisturbed country areas examples are still found of ancient yew avenues.

Unlike other conifers, the yew produces no cones. It is known to be deadly, for its leaves and fresh seeds contain a poison called Taxin.

Because the seed-making process of the yew is dependent upon the wind, it produces extraordinary amounts of pollen, which when released can cover large areas with its yellow dust. On warm spring days the air is filled with its golden shimmer.

CUSTOM & LEGEND

An old folk-tale tells why yews are 'dressed' so darkly. When the yew was a young species, in times when there were few people, it thought that all other trees were more beautiful, for their colourful leaves could flutter in the wind, unlike its stiff needles. The tree pined, thinking that the faeries had deliberately made it unattractive. Yet the faeries wanted to please the yew, and one sunny morning it found its needles had changed to leaves of gold and its heart danced with joy. But robbers came and stripped the tree bare, leaving it confused and sad. The faeries then gave it leaves of purest crystal and the yew loved its sparkle, but a storm of hail fell and the crystals shattered. Then it was given broad leaves and it waved them in the air, only for them to be eaten by goats. At this the yew gave up, for it realized that its original dress was the best, for it was of permanence, of long ages and deep knowledge, and in this the tree found comfort.

There are many tales about yews springing into growth upon the graves of lovers. In Irish legend the graves of Deidre and Naoise were staked with yew branches by the High King Conchobar in order to separate them. Yet the stakes grew into yew trees which wove their branches together above the graves and joined the lovers even in death.

Two yew trees sprouted out of the graves of the tragic lovers Tristan and Iseult. At their full height the yews reached their branches towards each other across the nave and intertwined so intensely they could nevermore be parted.

The yew was revered as a sacred tree, and the custom of the first Christian missionaries to preach under and erect churches near yews was a continuance of the ancient druidic practice of associating the yew with a place of burial adjacent to a place of worship.

In Christian terms the yew came to symbolize resurrection and it was used in church at Easter and on Palm Sunday. Shoots of yew were put into the shrouds of the dead, for it was believed to protect and restrain their spirits. The Church also thought that the yew protected against evil influences interfering with the shades of the dead.

Other associations between the yew and churchyards were formed when armies met at churches for blessings before battle, and English archers gathered yew branches from the churchyard trees to make their famous long-bows. It is said that many kings ordered the planting of yews in churchyards specifically for this purpose.

HEALING

Warning: It must be stressed that no one should self-administer yew. It is very poisonous and will cause death.

Culpeper states that the yew's poisonous qualities rise by distillation into the most active vegetable poison in the world, which acts upon the nervous system and destroys vital functions, but does not bring on sleep like opium or other poisons. Yew's Latin name, *Taxus*, is derived from the Greek *toxon*, meaning 'bow'. The connection of the tree to poison formed the derivative 'toxin', which was given to poisons in general. Recent discoveries about the yew are exciting, for the chemical properties of *Taxus* are believed to contain a formula, Taxol, which is an anti-cancer drug.

In homoeopathy a tincture of young yew shoots and berries (not the seed) is used for treating cystitis, headache, neuralgia, dimness of vision, affections of the heart and kidneys, gout and rheumatism.

MAGIC & INSPIRATION

Because the yew is an evergreen tree of extreme longevity, the ancient custom of mourners putting sprigs of yew into shrouds and graves of the departed showed they believed death was not the end of life, but merely a passing through into the continuance of life to come.

The yew is most powerful in midwinter, for it represents the passage of the sun through the darkest time of the year. Along with other evergreens it was revered as a tree of light, its green foliage in the dead of winter emphasizing that life would continue. To enhance this, all evergreens were traditionally dressed with shiny, sparkling objects at Yuletide, to attract the light of the sun back into the year.

In the cold regions of the north wind the yew is associated with faerie wildmen and Pictish deities, most of whom are said to have the ability to conjure up a faerie darkness in order to disappear. This may well have reference to the yew's ability to make things invisible for protection.

PHYSICAL USES

Yew sticks were cast by the Celts to divine the future. Yew rods were used for making written ogham scripts, because when the wood is seasoned and polished it has an extraordinary power of resisting decay. For this reason magical wands of yew are considered especially potent. When used positively, a wand or staff is a great healing implement, able to transform illness to health and sadness to joy.

Yew was included in the church decorations at Easter as a symbol of the continuity of life.

THE HOLLY

IRISH/GAELIC	*Tinne*
OGHAM	ᚆ
RUNIC	↑
RULING PLANET	Mars
ABILITIES	Strong protective herb. Clear wisdom and courage. Dream magic. To do with the element of Fire.
SEASON	Midwinter
HOLLY	*Ilex aquifolium*. Evergreen. POISONOUS (berries).

The holly is an evergreen shrub or small tree which gains heights of 30–40 feet (9–12 metres). It often branches from the top to the bottom of its trunk and needs little sun, for its leaves reflect light like a mirror. Holly is a native of Britain and central and southern Europe where it once helped form the great primeval forests.

Holly leaves are tough, leathery and heavily lobed, with each lobe ending in a very sharp spine. At heights above 12 feet (3½ metres) the leaves become less prickly and are often unlobed with just one sharp point at the end, for at this height the tree need not protect itself.

The holly blooms in May and most often the male and female flowers are on separate trees. Only the female flower changes into the holly berry and this can only happen if there is a male tree nearby from which pollen can be transferred. Pollination is encouraged by insects such as wild bees which are drawn to the flowers by the smell of the honey liquid released from their bases.

CUSTOM & LEGEND

The evergreen leaves of holly have represented immortality to mystics of all ages. To the druids the holly was especially sacred. When winter descended they advised people to take it into their homes, for then it would shelter the elves and faeries who could at this time join mortals without causing injury to them.

Since early times holly has been regarded as a plant of good omen, for its evergreen qualities make it appear invulnerable to the passage of time as the seasons change. It therefore symbolizes the tenacity of life even when surrounded by death, which it keeps at bay with strong protective powers.

Gifts of holly were given during the five-day Roman festival of Saturnalia, which celebrated the birth of the sun-god and culminated at the Winter Solstice. The power of these pagan celebrations on or about 22 December and their effect on the people were well recognized by the Church, and so they closely aligned the birth of Christ, 25 December, to the pagan date.

One of the strongest legendary images we have of holly is that of the holly king, symbolized by a giant man covered in holly branches, who carried a holly bush as his club. He is twinned with the oak king, and they become dual counterparts of the Nature god in his earth-protecting cycle and role. So powerful was the ancient symbology expressed by these concepts that the Church could not eradicate it from the minds of the people. Even though ritual enactment of pagan concepts was banned, mummers' plays evolved, using festive characters to veil sacred lore. Within these plays it was customary for the oak and holly kings to tussle for the hand of a fair maiden (the goddess). At midsummer the oak king was defeated by the holly king, at midwinter the oak king overpowered the holly king, expressing the seasonal tides.

Holly is especially lucky for men, and if they carry a leaf or berry it is said they quickly become attractive to women. In the north of Britain prickly holly leaves are called 'he-holly' and the smooth ones 'she-holly'. An old country saying states that if smooth-leaved holly is brought into the house first at yuletide the wife will rule the household the coming year, and if prickly holly enters first, the husband will rule.

HEALING

Warning: holly berries purge, but often cause nausea and vomiting. They are poisonous to children.

Most of holly's healing qualities are on the subtle planes, where by its presence or by taking its remedies it helps us transform our 'prickly' bits and improves our reaction to the world.

The Bach Flower Remedies use holly to treat oversensitivity, hatred, anger and aggressive behaviour.

An infusion of fresh or dried holly leaves is used to treat catarrhal coughs and bronchitis, pneumonia, influenza, rheumatism and fevers. In earlier days holly leaves were soaked in vinegar and put on corn for a day and a night in order to cure them. Chilblains were thrashed with a holly branch in order to 'chase the chill out'.

To enable wise decisions to be made before a course of action, holly can be used to meditate with or upon, to calm the mind and body of emotions.

MAGIC & INSPIRATION

On magical levels holly was regarded as an excellent herb of protection, specifically guarding against evil spirits, poisons, short-tempered or angry elementals, and thunder and lightning. The protection against lightning has been verified, for it has been shown that the spikes of holly leaves act like miniature lightning conductors, giving the trees immunity.

In the Irish/Gaelic ogham alphabet holly is called *Tinne*, a word believed to have originally meant 'fire'. From this was derived the word 'tinder', which *Chambers Twentieth Century Dictionary* describes as 'dry inflammable matter used for kindling fire from a spark'. This association of holly and fire has been known since ancient days when charcoal made from holly wood was used by armourers to forge swords and axe-heads. In continuation of this, holly is still used today as an incense in the ritual consecration of magical knives.

One of our best-known Christmas carols is 'The Holly and the Ivy'. Yet few people realize that it has its roots in paganism, where the holly and ivy represent the male and female principles of life. These were traditionally celebrated at the four quarters of the year, namely midwinter, the Spring Equinox, midsummer and the Autumn Equinox. At Yule it was the custom to dress a boy in the foliage of prickly holly and a girl in entwining ivy. Then, to lead the old solar year into the new, the holly-boy and ivy-girl paraded hand in hand throughout the community. This symbolized the god and goddess taking the evergreen quality of Nature through the darkest time of the year, encouraging the sun and the growth of vegetation.

'Of all the trees that are in the wood the holly bears the crown' reveals not only the importance of the tree, but also of the solar and lunar cycles and their reflection on earth. It also refers to the guardian qualities of holly, wherein it guides the precious energies of life. Royal work indeed!

PHYSICAL USES

Holly wood is ivory white and close-grained, and was prized in earlier days for its ability to take colour through staining, especially blue, green and red. When stained black it was styled the poor man's ebony. It was used extensively to inlay furniture with marquetry. The natural whiteness of the wood allowed it to be used for knife handles that resemble ivory. It was also traditionally valued for safeguarding door sills and handles. Holly was also used to make wooden spear shafts which gave balance and a good sense of direction. It is said that ancient chariot wheels contained holly wood, and it was used in much the same way in cart and coach wheels in later times.

Rabbits love to eat holly bark and it can be used as a tonic for rabbits kept in hutches. If you gather it yourself, ensure that only a little bark is taken from each tree and do *not* ring the tree (by removing bark all the way round) for it will die.

THE PINE

IRISH/GAELIC NAME	*Ailim*
OGHAM	+
RUNIC	∧
RULING PLANET	Mars
ABILITIES	Foresight. Long sight. Purification. Births. Incense. To do with the element of Air.
SEASONS	Winter; Spring
SCOT'S PINE	*Pinus sylvestris*. Coniferous. Evergreen.

Conifers hold age records as one of the oldest plant families. They are direct descendants of the primeval forests which flourished long before broadleaves. The Scot's pine is one of Britain's three native needle-leaved evergreens, along with juniper and yew. The silver fir was introduced from northern Europe in 1603. Pine trees like to grow in company with silver birch. Fly agaric, the *Aminita muscaria* mushroom, is common to both trees.

Pine is a straight tall tree, reaching heights of 100 feet (30 metres) and girths of 10–15 feet (3–4½ metres). It reaches ages of 600 years. Its strong tap-root helps it withstand high winds, and its beautiful colouring is best seen amongst the heather and bracken of moor and highland. If a pine tree is well situated in a bright open space it will begin reproduction after 20 years.

Pine forms pairs of leaves and this distinguishes it from yew and spruce which have leaves set singly in spirals on the branch, and from larch which has leaves in groups. That pine has leaves in the form of needles enables the tree to conserve and limit its water loss. This means that it is not reliant on moisture held in the soil and can thus grow in sandy soils.

In early spring the pine tree produces two kinds of single-sexed flowers. The male flowers are soft yellow fluffy 'knobs', clustering around the base of the season's new shoot of growth. The female flower is a tiny red bud-like object by the tip of the new spring shoot. On pollenation, the scales of the female flowers thicken at their tips and join together, sealed by resin.

By next spring this little flower-cone is bigger and pendulous. Towards the end of its second summer, or even the spring after that, the cone scales crack open and little brown seeds are revealed. Pine cones open only when it is dry so the wind-borne seeds have a chance to scatter and not drop wet to the tree's base. In autumn the empty cones fall from the branches, some two and a half years old. Three generations of cone can be found on a pine tree at any given time, sometimes all on a single branch, where new cones, fertilized and sealed cones, and empty cones stand one behind the other.

CUSTOM & LEGEND

In Egypt, Osiris, the great god of Egyptian magic, was seen as a tree-spirit in his primitive character and was represented ceremonially by the cutting down and hollowing out of a pine tree. Then an image of Osiris was made with the excavated wood from the tree and inserted back into the hollow tree. This was kept for a year to watch over the vines, and was then burned and scattered on the earth in order to fructify it for the next season's crop. His primitive character, felt to be embodied in a pine tree, also pointed to an alternative source of drink should the vines perish, for the resin of the Mediterranean pine itself is to this day a potent drink.

In Greek legend we are told how the pine became an evergreen. Rhea was the daughter of Uranus and Ge and the wife of Cronus. Under the name of Cybele she was loved by Atys, a Phrygian shepherd who vowed to be ever faithful to her. But he broke his vow and Cybele in anger changed him into a pine tree. Then, regretting her act, she wept beneath the branches. Zeus, her son, gave her comfort and promised that the pine would never lose its needles, and would stay green all through the year as a constant companion.

The pine is dedicated to Dionysus/Bacchus and in most representations of these gods a pine cone, phallic symbol of the god's fecundity, tips their thyrsus or wand.

The Greek goddess associated with pine is Pitthea. The god is Pittheus. As well as attributing pine with specific royal associations, the ancient Greeks gave crowns of pine to winners in the Isthmian Games.

In Europe druids burned great fires of pine at the Winter Solstice to draw back the sun and this practice became the custom of burning the Yule log. In many traditions pines and firs are associated with birth. Storks have always chosen such trees for their breeding nests and throughout the world legends tell us that storks carry the newborn to its parents. Pine's associations with birth and children does a lot to ease its somewhat dramatic reputation.

The Scot's pine is prolific in Britain. It is unique in that it is the sole northern European pine to have survived the Ice Age. However our great pine forests of yesteryear are but a memory, for man has taken heavily for his needs.

HEALING

Pine has always been recognized as a powerful bronchial disinfectant. It is very effective when used as an inhalant to ease respirational problems, as it specifically soothes irritations of the mucous membranes.

Pine also has uses as an antiseptic, an expectorant, a stimulant and a tonic, and it aids in the treatment of bladder and kidney problems. It has also been used as a treatment for gout and as a preparation to cure skin diseases.

Pine cones and needles are used in decoction, and are added to bath water to ease breathlessness, rheumatics and skin diseases. They are picked when green and fresh. Pine needles boiled in vinegar were once reputed to relieve toothache when packed around the tooth or when the liquid was swilled around the mouth. They were also used to heal 'green' wounds.

MAGIC & INSPIRATION

The resin of the pine tree, collected from cuts in its trunk which ooze the gummy substance, can be used as an incense gum which when burnt clears a place of negative energies. It can also be used as a 'counter-magic' incense, for it repels evil or spells cast against us by returning them to source.

To clear ourselves of negativity, pine needles or oil of pine can be added to our bath water. As we soak, we can concentrate on allowing negativity to float out of us into the water. Each dark thought, each ache or tension, each pain or discontent can be mentally pushed to the surface of our body and can be seen to flow out from us into the water, and thus, when the plug is pulled, down the drain.

Pine cones were traditionally used to tip the god's thyrsus in fertility rites. The fact that they are also phallic in appearance, especially when tipping a wand, gave added impetus to the fertility of the rite. Such wands are still used in Wiccan rites today.

As spring moves into early summer, pines shed clouds of pollen-dust into the air, often creating thick floating hazes on sunny days. In ancient days this dust was collected by druids for magical and theatrical purposes, as was yew pollen.

Pine pollen was also used in money spells, for its yellow colour was believed to attract gold. Sawdust of pine wood can be used as a base for any incenses used in money rituals.

Pine branches and sprays have always been used for protection, for when placed at doors and windows they were thought to keep out evil. When placed above a sick person's bed, pine branches aid recovery.

A natural pine wood grows to Nature's plan, forming where the wind and birds have carried the seeds. It is very different from a man-made plantation, and this is felt in the atmosphere of the place, the way the light expresses itself and the feelings given off by the trees.

The richness of pine's colouring and its proud poise set it apart from any other tree, and it is always expressive, no matter how grey the day. The bark is a rich earthy red, giving the tree a glow of warmth, and it flakes off the tree like butterfly wings in hues of salmon pink and green. Pine needles are also provocative and to handle a resinous spray of pine intoxicates the senses.

PHYSICAL USES

Many products are collected from pine. Its resin was once used for sealing-wax and to improve violin bows by adding resonance to their sound. It was used to coat the insides of beer casks and was known as 'brewer's pitch'. Its oil or tar also forms the 'pitch' used medicinally by veterinarians as an antiseptic, and its resin was used as pitch to seal boats and was reckoned to give them magical protection. In the Mediterranean the resin of the sabina pine gives distinctive flavour to the popular retsina wines.

Pine trees have good trunks which produce quick-growing wood. When sawn, pine timber is yellowish in colour and is fairly soft and slightly resinous. In the past it was mainly used for pit props and rough building work, and in more modern times for railway sleepers and telegraph poles.

THE HAZEL

IRISH/GAELIC	*Coll*
OGHAM	ᚉ
RUNIC	ᚲ
RULING PLANET	Mercury (nuts); Sun (plant)
ABILITIES	Intuition. Divination. Dowsing. Wands. Individuality. The power to find that which is hidden. To do with the element of Air.
SEASONS	Spring (Imbolc); Autumn
HAZEL	*Corylus avellana*. Deciduous.

While hazel is usually a large shrub, it can grow to the size of a small tree. Hazel is plentiful in copses, oak woods and hedgerows. It is common throughout most of Britain, Europe, America, Africa, Turkey and western Asia and thrives in damp places near ponds or streams, though it fruits better if the land has drainage. It has various species to its family.

The bark of the hazel is smooth and light brown in colour. It is speckled with lighter brown lenticels, the pores of the tree, where the cells of the bark are drawn apart to let air pass to the inner tissue, allowing the tree to breathe. Hazel leaves open in early spring. They are a beautiful lime green in colour, grow singly on the branches and are a pointed oval, slightly heart-shaped and asymmetrical. They turn from their summer colour of mid-green to greeny-browns and pinks in the autumn.

Often as early as January, its male catkins, or 'lamb's tails', leave behind their stiff winter brownness as they grow and fill with pollen, becoming like tassels of gold which hang vividly against the dark bareness of the winter branches. They shed pollen to the wind long before the first appearance of leaf and flower on the land, save perhaps the snowdrop.

The female flowers are small, with red styles which look

like small crimson brushes. Once the hazel's pollination is complete, the male catkins fade, their work done.

The hazelnuts are ripe by September and can be eaten straight from the tree. The shape of the leafy frills around them distinguishes the hazel species. Hazelnuts keep for thousands of years in petrified form and many (hard and black as jet) are found in ancient bogland.

CUSTOM & LEGEND

The most prolific legends concerning hazel come from Ireland. A king named Mac Coll, meaning 'Son of Hazel', was one of the three earliest rulers in Ireland. Mac Coll was one of the last kings of the Tuatha de Danaan. The hazel tree from which he took his name and power was specifically associated with wisdom.

Druidic legends concerning Connla's Well tell of the salmon of wisdom. This father of all salmon, when first going to sea, was drawn to the magical well and his journeyings thence instilled in all future salmon their migratory genes. On reaching the well the salmon was given the great gift of wisdom by the well's guardians, for each of the nine hazel trees surrounding the well dropped a sacred hazelnut into the water. On swallowing these nuts the salmon became the recipient of all knowledge.

Druidic legend also tells of Fionn, a pupil of a chief druid who lived on the River Boyne. The druid master intended to eat the salmon of knowledge which he had caught in a deep pool, for its flesh, it was said, 'would make him conscious of everything that was happening in Ireland'. Young Fionn was told to cook the salmon for his master, but not to taste it. Yet while he cooked the fish he burnt his thumb and automatically put it into his mouth for relief. Thus it was Fionn who received the salmon's gift of farsight, 'seeing all that was happening in the High Courts of Tara'. This story has a Welsh equivalent in the legend of Cerridwen and Gwion.

The Roman god Mercury and the Greek god Hermes both carried a staff of hazel, sometimes depicted with two ribbons attached to it, to show its speed through the air. Often these ribbons were shown as snakes intertwining along the staff, forming the caduceus symbol of the healing arts used by healers and physicians to this day.

Thus the spirit of the hazel is strongly aligned to speed through the air as well as through water, and in its legendary links with the sacred salmon we see possibly the birth of both these elemental associations, for salmon swim exceedingly fast in water and then leave the waters in mighty leaps, appearing to fly through the air.

In Wales supple hazel twigs were woven into 'wishing-caps' which granted the desire of the wearer. Pilgrim's staffs were made from hazel and so attached did the owners become to them that they were buried alongside them after death.

HEALING

As the tree of immortality hazel was especially revered, and because its nuts were believed to contain all wisdom they were in themselves talismans for a healthy life. Hazel was esteemed as a plant of great virtue, said to have the power to cure fevers, diarrhoea and excessive menstrual flow.

An old country charm to prevent toothache was to carry a double hazelnut in the pocket, and a cross of hazel wood laid on a snake-bite was said to draw out the poison.

The kernels of the hazelnut, mixed with mead or honeyed water, are good for coughs which will not clear. Mixed with pepper in decoction they clear the head.

The greatest healing provided by hazel is found within its atmosphere. Being near hazel trees or meditating upon a piece of hazel brings the spirit alive and allows us to quickly cast off the old and move on to the new. Hazel's atmosphere exudes exhilaration and inspiration.

MAGIC & INSPIRATION

Hazel has always been regarded as magical for its presence inspires our intuitional senses. It was called the 'poet's tree', for in the minds of the ancients it had great associations with faerie lore and supposedly allowed entrance into such realms.

Druids carried rods made from hazel to gain poetic and magical inspiration and, under certain conditions, druids used hazel to invoke invisibility.

The hazel is powerful in early spring when its energy and sap are surging outward, and in autumn, when its energy is contained within its harvest of magical nuts. Such timings should be noted when cutting wands or staffs. Traditionally hazel twigs and forks for divining should be cut on Midsummer's Eve in order for them to be at their most powerful.

Hazel can be used at all times for protection. Its ruling planets, the Sun and Mercury, make it a brilliant healing plant.

As shown by its legends and by its preference for growing in damp places, hazel is strongly associated with the qualities of water. Thus on many levels it has great association with the moon, controller of the tides on earth.

The epitome of hazel energy, the movement and the emotion and the visuals, is shown by the magical salmon, the 'flying-fish' which leaps from the water in pure exhilaration, like flashing quicksilver. Ancient druids observed Nature closely and such association was exemplified in their teachings and legends.

However, druidic teachings also tell us how the hazel could transform itself for defence, for if necessary it became gnarled and leafless, dripping poisonous milk, and was known as the 'dripping hazel'. In this context, those who attempted to enter the highest magical realms, if they had not truth within their hearts would face such a guardian, which no doubt fed upon the bones of profanity!

PHYSICAL USES

The hazel's spreading roots allow man to reap great rewards by coppicing the tree. The long straight shoots that coppiced hazels send up from the ground are pliable and difficult to break. They are used in various ways, for basket-making, hoops and hurdles, fishing rods and walking sticks.

Hazel rods are still used to dowse for water. It was also used for dowsing mineral ores and it has been said that its liking for certain minerals draws it to them.

A horse which had overeaten could be aided by binding its legs and feet to hazel rods, and by whispering certain words into its right ear. Tying hazel twigs onto a horse's harness was a traditional way of protecting horses from enchantment by fairies. At lambing time hazel catkins were placed around the kitchen fireplace to aid the births and as they resemble lamb's tails, as already mentioned, this act could be viewed as one of sympathetic magic.

THE BLACK-THORN

IRISH/GAELIC	*Straif*
OGHAM	ᚎ
RUNIC	ᛀ
RULING PLANETS	Saturn (plant); Mars (fruit)
ABILITIES	Cleansing. Karmic issues. Lack of choice but with hope rising from the depths. To do with the element of Fire.
SEASONS	Spring (Imbolc); Late Autumn (Samhain)
BLACKTHORN	*Prunus spinosa*. Deciduous.

Blackthorn grows densely in hedgerows, woods and thickets throughout Britain, most often in the company of the gentler hawthorn. It is typically a crooked little tree or shrub, with many thorny angular branches and black or dark brown knobbly twigs.

The strong thorns are long sharp spines which can give painful stabs and scratches which usually turn septic.

In blossoming so early, even before its own leaves are out, blackthorn defies the still-cold northern winds that continue to grip the land in winter. Its small flowers are five-petalled, star-shaped and abundant. Small white buds like little white balls intersperse giant clusters of newly opened blossom. The leaves of the blackthorn are neat small oval shapes of a dark matt-green colour. The blackthorn is deciduous and sheds its yellowed leaves by winter. Then the massed shape of its knobbly branches is revealed.

Blackthorn fruit are called sloes. They develop from the flower and transform from a green hard state to soft plum-shaped purply-black fruit with a silvery-blue bloom. They are more or less inedible because of their dry acrid taste and are mainly used as a 'bitter' in drinks.

CUSTOM & LEGEND

By tradition blackthorn was regarded as a sister of the hawthorn. The customs attached to fertility celebrations used the qualities of both plants to great effect, particularly the erotic ones with which fertility was evoked. When blackthorn was used in the Mayday celebrations, it topped the maypole entwined in a hawthorn garland and, like beech, was called the 'Mother of Woods'. As sister trees blackthorn and hawthorn are also linked in Christian legend, for blackthorn was said to bloom at midnight on Christmas Eve, as did the miraculous hawthorn known as the Glastonbury Thorn. Both plants were also believed to have formed the crown of thorns, a belief which did much to overlay them with superstition.

At new year, when people gathered together to celebrate, crowns of blackthorn were made and ritually burned as firecharms, so their scattered ashes could fertilize the fields. Blackthorn crowns or garlands were also used to wassail the apple trees and when mistletoe was woven into the garlands they were hung up to bring luck in the coming year.

Unfortunately blackthorn also has a grim reputation, for its thorns were used by people who took chances to seize power by harming others. As already explained, a scratch often leaves wounds that turn septic, and if, as legend tells us, such thorns were also tipped with poison, we can well imagine the death-blow they dealt. When the blackthorn was used thus it was called the 'pin of slumber'.

Even more unfortunate were the superstition and paranoia of the witch panic throughout Britain and Europe. Rumour asserted that the devil himself pricked his initiates on the fingers with thorns and many 'witches' were searched for the 'devil's mark'. This eventually became the label of any mark found on the body of any suspected person, and was deemed enough evidence for a death sentence. So strong were the associations thought to exist between witches and blackthorn, it was reputedly one of the woods used to burn witches on the pyres. Such usage was meant to deliver a final insult to the victim.

Because of all the secrecy attached to such actions, blackthorn became known as the 'increaser and keeper of dark secrets'. While we may acknowledge this, we will hopefully realize in the following pages that blackthorn also has a positive quality which cleanses and prepares us for personal progress and development.

HEALING

The fruit of the blackthorn is very astringent, and for this reason in the seventeenth and eighteenth centuries thick brews of unripe sloes were used to treat 'fluxes in the belly', and as strong purgatives. In purifications and cleansings the thorns represent our negative attitudes which rend and tear at us and our lives, and which we need to cast off if we want to be happy and creative. By using blackthorn in meditation, or even by just having it around, we can begin such a process.

The wintry blackthorn specifically deals with the deep psychic levels. A word of caution should be brought in here though, for the purgative nature of the blackthorn and its winter fruit means that its action can be harsh and unrelenting. For those who need a gentler process, the spring blackthorn with its massed white blossoms provides a lighter cleansing.

MAGIC & INSPIRATION

The growing warmth and light of the sun fill every living thing with vital energy which peaks into full-frontal fertility by Mayday. To express this blackthorn blossoms were traditionally woven into the hawthorn crowns which topped the phallic maypoles. Blackthorn wishing-wands were also used at this time for divination and obtaining desires.

While the Imbolc blackthorn helps us burst through our wintry state and the Mayday blackthorn enhances our communal sexual spirit in the full throes of spring, the Samhain blackthorn guides individuals through the darkening weeks to the Winter Solstice. Here we can compare the human passage with that of the mythical sun-god, for like him we too enter the Underworld, in terms of our unconscious realms, as the sun completes its cycle. We also face the same initiatory process, that is, overcoming our negative selves in order to facilitate rebirth.

According to legend the sun-god received help from the trees – a talismanic branch from a specific species of tree enabling him to escape his Underworld confines. There are many trees which help in this process, and each species is concerned with specific areas of mind and body. Blackthorn allows us burst through and cleanse our blockages caused by negativity. This gains us a clearer entrance into our inner worlds and the ability to survive the facing thereof.

In the context of personal relationships, blackthorn tells us of respect, of not crossing lines beyond which we will inflict pain. How often do we forget respect and stab at our loved ones in anger or frustration; how often do we throw trust to the winds to make a point or revel in our power over another's weaknesses? If we are honest, we are all capable of it, especially when we ourselves are in pain.

Yet blackthorn is not all about pain, for our ancestors used its blossom in fertility rites, where its erotic perfume helped evoke love. Thus the true message given by the blackthorn is that by understanding and calming our emotions, and by being aware of the capacity of our negativity, we can ease our own suffering and eventually the suffering of the world. Thus we can come to love the mystery that is life.

PHYSICAL USES

The wood of the blackthorn is very tough. It was used to make the teeth of rakes, as well as for cudgels and sticks used for fighting at fairs. When made into a walking stick and highly polished, it reveals a dark rich shine.

Blackthorn is useful to the farmer. It is a good hedgerow plant, its spines protecting the young foliage from browsing animals, as well as forming a strong barrier.

Sloes give the strongest natural red dye, which has always been used by country people. As sloes are very astringent they were added to drinks as 'bitters' and were used in jam-making. Sloe juice was used as a marking ink.

Sloe gin, which is very potent, is possibly the best known use for the fruit of the blackthorn.

THE
SILVER
BIRCH

IRISH/GAELIC	*Beith*
OGHAM	┣
RUNIC	↓
RULING PLANET	Venus
ABILITIES	Healing. New starts and beginnings. Mysteries of the young goddess. To do with the elements of Air and Water.
SEASONS	Spring; Autumn
SILVER BIRCH	*Betula alba (Pendula)*. Deciduous.

Besides being one of the daintiest trees the silver birch is the hardiest of all broadleaves, a native of Iceland, Greenland, Britain and most of the northern hemisphere. It is an extremely feminine tree and is easily recognized by the tracery of its delicate twigs and branches.

Birches can live to be 100 years old. They root near the surface and prefer light and moist soils. The earth beneath a birch tree is lush and welcoming to flowers, and the tree's affinity with water encourages the growth of many forms of fungi.

'Burelles' of twigs may appear high in the crown of some trees, looking like old birds' nests. These are called 'witch's knots' in Scotland and are made by insects which lay their eggs in the tree. The defence mechanism of the tree then overproduces in that area and 'glues' the excessive twig growth together.

The silvery-white bark is thin and paper-like and peels off the trunk to reveal an inner bark of russet brown. The dark transverse markings on the tree's trunk are lenticels, spaces where air is let into the living tissues beneath the bark. Birch bark does not rot, and if a tree is blown down and left, all the inner wood decays but the bark remains intact in a hollow tube.

New birch leaves appear at the beginning of spring and are ace of spades shape, small and very pointed, with double-toothed edges. They are a delicate light green colour, touched with yellow and tinged with a pink underside which can show through to their upper leaf. Because of their slender stalks they move on the gentlest of winds.

Birch has both male and female flowers on the same tree. The female flowers are small erect catkins. They await the touch of pollen from the male catkins, by means of insects and wind.

By July the seeds have become light brown and hang, still clustered in a catkin shape, waiting for the wind to make them airborne. In autumn, when all the seeds are finally taken from the tree by the wind, the young male catkins for next year appear on the tip of each new shoot.

CUSTOM & LEGEND

The silver birch is known as the 'Lady of the Woods'. It is womanly, constant and friendly, a tree of enchantment. When seen by moonlight it presents its most outstanding feature, a gleaming silvery bark, which legends throughout Europe describe as the hallmark of faerie.

As birch is one of the first trees to leaf in spring it is known as the tree of inception. It is also seen as a tree of purification, cleansing the old to make way for the new. At the ancient Beltaine festivities birch twigs were used to light the oak fires and traditionally the Mayday love-making was enjoyed in a birch wood or forest.

In Irish legend the lovers Diarmid, King of All Ireland, and the goddess Grainne made their home in shelters of birch twigs as they fled from their pursuer, Finn Mac Coll. The lovers are said to have also slept each night beside a fresh dolmen. They journeyed throughout the west of Ireland and their numerous bed-places are still recognized by people in those areas.

An old Welsh custom was for a man to give a birch garland to the woman he loved and she gave a similar one back if she felt the same affection.

In many parts of Britain and Europe birch was anciently used as a living maypole at Beltaine. Conversely, in Scandinavian legend the birch was regarded as the tree around which the last battle for worldly existence would be fought.

Being a white tree, the silver birch was seen to have the ability to ward off evil or negative spirits. Traditionally birch rods were used to drive out the spirit of the old year and for beating the bounds of a parish. They were also used in the none too kind practice of beating spirits and demons out of lunatics. The Romans carried birch rods when they installed their consuls, no doubt to beat back the crowds in an early use of caning.

Birch is also associated with the spirits of the dead and mourners, for the tree was seen to be in sympathy by its pendulous habit of 'weeping'.

When used for the first ogham inscription in Ireland the birch became associated with the sun-god Lugh, for this first inscription warned him that his wife was being taken away to the land of faerie.

HEALING

Water collected from the birch tree is called 'birch blood' as well as 'birch water'. In some parts of Europe country people still lay in a supply in the spring before the trees leaf. A sweet fizzy wine can be made from birch water and it is also used medicinally to prevent stones in the kidneys or bladder. It is invaluable for treating rheumatic diseases or for use as a cleansing mouthwash. It cures skin of spots, fades freckles, and is used to clear scurf and heal acne.

Birch bark is diuretic, antiseptic and a tonic, and it contains an anaesthetic which causes nerve-endings to lose sensation, making us less aware of pain. If applied externally, putting the wet fresh internal side of the bark against the skin, muscle pain can be relieved.

Gypsies use birch bark for treating eczema and a decoction of bark treats intermittent fevers. The bark should be collected in late spring and early summer, taking care not to ring around the tree, for it will die.

The young leaves are used for treating cystitis and other infections of the urinary system, removing excess water and 'flushing' the body. A decoction of birch leaves made into a tea greatly increases the output of urine from the body. It also dissolves kidney-stones and gives great relief from rheumatism and gout.

Rheumatic and arthritic pains are eased if a warm bed is filled with birch leaves, for they induce a heavy sweat and bring the patient relief.

MAGIC & INSPIRATION

Because birch casts off malignancy and allows a fresh start, it was often used at Samhain, the start of the Celtic year, when purification was believed to be essential. The dried leaves of birch were also used to 'charm' a baby's cot, giving the child inside strength to cast off any weakness and gain the best start in life.

According to legend, all respect should be shown to the birch tree, for if this Lady of the Woods finds you maligning trees, anger rises in her whip-like branches. Always ask if you need something from the trees, especially if you want to take the bark. Birch bark makes exceptionally potent magical parchment.

The deities associated with silver birch are mostly love- and fertility-goddesses. In northern Europe, where the birch is profuse, Frigga represented married love, and Freya was the Norse goddess of love and fecundity. The goddess Arianrhod was invoked through the birch tree for her aid in births and initiations. Closer to home, Eostre, the Anglo-Saxon goddess of spring, was evoked and celebrated around and through the birch tree between the Spring Equinox and Beltaine. The silver birch is used in all works of love, protection and purification, for it contains the caring qualities of the feminine.

The silver birch is the most faerie-like of all our trees. It is light and airy with foliage and branches which dance upon the breeze, and its atmosphere allows us to relax from the pressures of the workaday world and become reinvigorated.

The fertility associations of the birch are reflected in the courting of the god and goddess. The Gaelic name for birch, *beith*, also means 'inception' or 'beginning', and while this alludes to the beginning of the light season, it is also descriptive of the courtship of the earth and sun which grows and culminates throughout the solar year.

PHYSICAL USES

Birch is grown in northern Europe to produce plywood for furniture-making and in northern countries birch bark is used for roofing, baskets, cord, woven shoes, nets, plates, torches (when rolled up), parchment and paper. Birch bark is water-resistant because it contains large quantities of resin. In Norway, for weatherproof roofing a layer of earth is placed over a bark-laid base. In Lapland the bark is also used for cloaks and leggings. It burns well when everything else is wet and this is more or less the only way to destroy it.

Birch bark is like paper and from time immemorial it has been used to write upon. In the north, after the bark has been stripped off a birch tree, the wood is used for the Yule log.

Native North Americans use birch bark in the making of canoes. A birch bark canoe is ribbed with cedar and bound with larch roots, and its seams are made watertight with pine resin.

In Sweden and Lapland birch sap replaces sugar, and in Scandinavia farmers use the leafing time of the birch to gauge the sowing of their wheat.

THE
APPLE
TREE

IRISH/GAELIC	*Quert*
OGHAM	ᚊ
RUNIC	K
RULING PLANET	Venus
ABILITIES	Healing. Love. Poetic inspiration. Works of destiny. Foundation. To do with the element of Water.
SEASONS	All
APPLE	*Pyrus malus* or *communis*. Deciduous.

The wild crab-apple is Britain's only indigenous apple tree. It is small and beautiful; a delightful tree, especially when in flower or fruit.

In ancient days there were some 22 varieties of apple world-wide according to Pliny, but it was not until the eighteenth century that hybrids appeared in Britain from Europe, in particular from France. There are now thought to be about 2,000 species of apple world-wide.

The crab-apple belongs to the rose family, along with hawthorn, wild pear and blackthorn, and like these it also has thorns which develop from spurs on its branches. Old apple trees are the commonest trees to host mistletoe and as such were sacred in druidic lore.

The trunks of old crab-apple trees become very aged and gnarled-looking. The trees often lean at crazy angles, as they try to hide themselves amongst other trees in hedgerows and the fringes of woods. The leaves are almost heart-shaped, mid-green and somewhat glossy. The crab-apple's flower-buds open in April and May to reveal small flowers tinged with deep pink which smell very similar to the flowers of honeysuckle. As with cultivated apples, cross pollination is also necessary for a good crop of crab-apples.

By autumn the bunches of delicate little crab-apples have ripened to yellow and red and measure about an inch

(2½ cm) across. They are broader than they are long, with deep depressions at either end of the core, and they hang on long stalks. Some crab trees hold fruit on their branches throughout winter and are a marvellous sight on grey days.

CUSTOM & LEGEND

Within Greek myths the apple orchards of Paradise were known as the Garden of the Hesperides. In this garden there grew an especially sacred apple tree whose fruit conferred immortality. It was tended and guarded by nine fair maidens, the Hesperides themselves, who were representatives of Aphrodite, the goddess of love, whose symbol is the apple. These maidens symbolically joined hands around the sacred tree and became its outer protection, along with a serpent which coiled around its roots.

Heracles' eleventh labour was to fetch fruit from this specific tree but the theft of the apples from the divine garden caused great consternation in the heavens. Eventually Heracles gave the apples to the goddess Athene and she returned them to the Hesperides. Such tests or labours are found in ancient myths the world over. The most famous in Britain was linked to Llew (Lugh), who asked the Sons of Tuirenn to acquire for him the apples which 'grow in the Garden of Light over an ocean'.

In Western legend the apple orchards of Paradise were known as 'the Isles of the Blessed' and they housed the Tree of Knowledge upon which three sacred apples grew. The serpent which guarded the tree and its sacred apples was seen as the goddess Cerridwen, guarding the knowledge of the seasons.

It is very noticeable how the Biblical legend of the Garden of Eden adapted this theme. The serpent became representative of all evil, woman became the tempter and the apple became the symbolic fruit of the downfall of man from grace.

In Irish legend there was a magical Silver Bough cut from a mystical apple tree and upon this bough hung nine apples which played incessant music which lulled people into a deep trance-like sleep. In Celtic times apples were considered food of the gods, and by tradition apple trees have been wassailed over the centuries by druids and country people to ensure good crops. Wassailing is a seasonal ceremony in which blessings and prayers are said to the trees.

According to Norse myth, apples were given to the gods by humans in order that the gods might help them and keep old age at bay. Apple wood is still seen as an emblem of security and a symbol of poetic immortality. Felling an apple tree has always been said to bring bad luck and in earlier days it brought the death penalty. To burn an apple tree is considered sacrilege indeed.

HEALING

Apples are filled with strong therapeutic agents: sugars, amino-acids, vitamins, malic and tartaric acids, pectin and numerous mineral salts. They can be prescribed for infections of the intestine, constipation, mental and physical overstrain, fatigue, hypertension, rheumatism, gout, anaemia, bronchial diseases, urine retention, hepatic insufficiency, demineralization, gastric and kidney conditions, hoarseness, coughs and excess cholesterol in the blood. They are best eaten first thing in the morning and last thing at night, when they encourage sleep. Grated raw apple can be eaten slowly when you wake in the morning to prevent morning sickness in pregnancy.

Raw apple can be made into a poultice for inflamed eyes, badly healing wounds and aches and pains. A compress of the pulp or the juice restores skin tissue and warts can be cured by rubbing them with two halves of an apple which are then buried. As the apple decays the warts disappear.

MAGIC & INSPIRATION

The apple has always been regarded as the possessor of amazing healing and magical qualities. It is a symbol of beauty and fruitfulness. Apples have been used for love, immortality and healing spells, and were capable, legend tells us, of healing severely wounded men in battles past.

Traditional customs defended apple trees against bad weather and pieces of coral were hung in the trees' branches to give extra protection, along with the wassailing. A traditional time of planting apple trees was May-eve. Small pieces of coal were placed beneath their roots and a good libation of cider 'watered' them in.

At midsummer, as apple trees are the most common bearers of the sacred mistletoe, they were paid homage by the druids, and the giver of the mistletoe was revered as the goddess of the apple orchard.

Apples are specifically used at the Samhain festivities to ensure that the correct atmosphere of trust and friendship ensues. Samhain is the time when the light half of the year moves into the dark, and the eating of apples at this time also helps us make the corresponding internal changes, lining us up spiritually and magically.

Many apple games, such as 'bobbing' for apples floating in cauldrons of water, enliven celebrations at this time. The atmosphere is also enhanced by apple juice flowing from the ritual cup. As the apple is known as both the food of the gods and the food of the dead, and as the apple bough was believed to be the talisman which enabled gods and heroes to rise from the Underworld, altars are piled high with them at Samhain.

Apples are sacred to the love-goddesses, and any rituals or gatherings of people are enhanced by their presence or use. Many love spells and charms are worked with apples. A simple act of love magic is to share an apple with a friend, for it is guaranteed to aid companionship. Apple blossoms are added to all love spells.

Apples are also an essential part of garden magic. Apple wood can be carved into talismans or amulets to attract love and longevity. It is excellent to carve into a magical wand or an image for specific healing or love spells.

The apple was one of the seven chieftain trees of Britain, and as such potently pagan. In Europe the juice of the apple was used in the druidic sacrament, much as the grape was used in sacrament to Dionysus/Bacchus in other lands.

PHYSICAL USES

The fruit of the apple tree is the part most used, though apple wood is beautifully grained when carved into small objects. The apple is a rich source of health-giving food and drink for humans, and is excellent for healing both the mind and the body. They have always been used as a symbol of harvest and form an integral part of the traditions of the land, being a strong link between Nature and the country people.

Lightning was said never to split an apple-tree trunk for it was protected by the great quality of love it contained. Because of this people were advised to plant apple trees near their homes, both as a protection against lightning and to generate love in the household.

Cider apples were the traditional mainstay of most farming communities, for the cider produced on farms refreshed farm workers and was a health-giving commodity.

Great pride is still taken in the qualities of cider produced, which are distinctive to each farm.

The sour fruits of the crab-apple are used in jellies, along with other fruit. Their juice makes an excellent substitute vinegar.

THE
HAWTHORN
TREE

IRISH/GAELIC	*Huathe*
OGHAM	┤
RUNIC	И
RULING PLANET	Mars
ABILITIES	Fertility. Guardian. Cleansing. Door to the Otherworld. Happiness. To do with the element of Fire.
SEASONS	Spring (Beltaine); Autumn
HAWTHORN	*Crataegus oxyacantha*. Deciduous.

The hawthorn is a small tree of the rose family. It can grow up to 30 feet (9 metres) high but is usually smaller and is more often than not broader than high. Given encouragement by man, it is very much a hedge-tree. 'Haw' is believed to mean 'hedge'. Hawthorn is more a village tree than a forest tree, for it seems to prefer to grow close to people.

Hawthorn is most often companion to blackthorn in the hedgerows, but the two are easily distinguishable, especially in spring, for blackthorn blossoms before leafing, and hawthorn blossoms along with its newly opened leaves. It grows quickly and sends out many side shoots and branches which make a sturdy impenetrable barrier to livestock, even though cattle and horses love to eat its leaves.

Unlike blackthorn, which sends out suckers, hawthorn does not have a large root system and is therefore not greedy with the soil's nutrients. This encourages many forms of plant life to grow in its vicinity.

In April the hawthorn's leaf-buds open and little bundles of pale green leaves appear on every branch. They are deeply divided into toothed lobes and become shiny green on top and grey-green below.

The flowers have five snow-white petals set around slender stamens with bright pink heads. With its mass of blossom and leaves, each branch becomes weighted down and the rich evocative scent of the flowers permeates the air. Hawthorn blossoms contain both male and female parts and are fertilized by insects crawling over them.

By summer the seeds will have grown into small green berries which are a shiny dark red by autumn. They hang in long-stalked bunches awaiting the attention of birds, which love to eat them. They then propagate the seeds upon their flights.

CUSTOM & LEGEND

In pagan terms hawthorn is a prime symbol of fertility. It was always the traditional tree used at marriages, for it reflects the union of the forces of Nature.

In ancient times there were many hawthorn cults ruled over by goddesses to whom the tree was sacred. In Britain one of the earliest hawthorn-goddesses was Olwen, daughter of Yspaddaden Pencawr, a wild man called Giant Hawthorn.

Another spring-goddess associated with hawthorn is Blodeuwedd who was magically created from nine kinds of spring flowers as a consort for Llew Llaw-Gywffes, a

Celtic sun-god. It is Blodeuwedd who the May Queen represents when she is dressed in blossoms at the Mayday festivities. The May King who courts the May Queen at the celebrations also wears hawthorn blossom in his leafy costume.

The most famous Christian legend concerning hawthorn is that of the Glastonbury Thorn. This sixteenth-century story tells us that as Christianity entered Britain the Celtic spirit was moved by the spirituality it expressed and that this was emphasized when Joseph of Arimathea came to Glastonbury. On Wearyall Hill he rested, leaning upon his staff, which during the night rooted into the ground and became a blossoming hawthorn tree. This was taken as a sign that the new religion of Christ was to be founded at Glastonbury, and Joseph and his 12 disciples built the first Christian chapel there.

Joseph's staff became known as the Glastonbury Thorn, which ever after blossomed on Christmas Day in honour of the divine birth of Christ. The original tree was said to be still living in Puritan days. To this day a blossoming twig from the Glastonbury Thorn is annually sent to the Queen at Christmas.

Christian legend also tells us that an eastern species of hawthorn, known as the Albiespyne, formed the crown of thorns used in the Crucifixion, and that because hawthorn had touched the Lord's brow it was sanctified.

The Italian goddess of hawthorn was Cardea, who presided over childbirth and protected infants. She was propitiated at weddings with hawthorn torches.

In European myth hawthorns are connected to miraculous conceptions. In Greek myth Hera conceived Ares and his twin-sister Eris when she touched hawthorn blossoms. However Ares was an Olympian god of war, and his sister Eris provoked many quarrels and became symbolic of the type of strife usually associated with blackthorn.

In Britain Henry VII claimed hawthorn as the badge of the House of Tudor, because at the Battle of Bosworth Field the crown of England was stolen from Richard III and hidden in a hawthorn bush.

HEALING

Hawthorn radiates qualities of growth and health. People have always approached it for healing, especially those trees that grow near wells and springs.

Modern science shows that hawthorn contains chemical components which are sedative, anti-spasmodic and diuretic, and this makes the plant a remarkable natural regulator of arterial blood pressure. Known as 'valerian of the heart', hawthorn is most valuable as a heart stimulant.

With its excellent sedative effects hawthorn also helps people who suffer from palpitations, angina pectoris, the menopause and any disturbance of the blood circulation.

Hawthorn flowers, made into a strong infusion of a good spoonful per cup, can be drunk two or three times a day at the onset of angina. A cupful of the same infusion can be taken at night to ease insomnia. The flowers are used in decoction to heal facial blemishes and acne.

Hawthorn berries ease diarrhoea and dysentery, kidney inflammations and disorders.

MAGIC & INSPIRATION

Beltaine is a festival of birth and bunches of flowering hawthorn were always carried in wedding processions to give fertility to the marrying couple and hope to their desires, while in Ireland newly married couples still dance around thorn bushes to gain extra blessings on their marriage. During May the strength of the rising sun's energy also gives impetus and effect to any healings performed with hawthorn.

Old Midsummer's Day falls on 5 July and at this time the hawthorn trees themselves were decorated. The custom of blessing and adorning thorn trees is called 'bawming the thorn'. Flower garlands and red ribbons are attached to a tree, then children dance around it.

Upon farmsteads the kitchen was given protection from fire by a charm created from hawthorn which was intimately connected to all aspects of village life, especially that conducted around village wells.

The hawthorn is associated with fulfilment in the hearts of the people, and its beautiful blossoms were thought to help prayers reach heaven. Sick children were traditionally carried to hawthorns where pagan prayers were said for their healing, and hawthorn blossoms were attached to a baby's cradle for similar healing and protection.

To carry a sprig of hawthorn was to have proof against storms at sea and lightning on shore, and in some regions hawthorn was taken into the home and placed in the rafters for protection against spirits, ghosts and storms.

To many country people and travellers throughout the ages, hawthorn is known as the 'bread and cheese' tree. This is because leaves eaten from the hawthorn were reckoned to give as much sustenance as a plate of bread and cheese. Upon long journeys, Nature's food picked from the trees and hedgerows gave travellers comfort and strength when they were far from habitation.

However, Britain's hedgerows contain hawthorn for reasons other than sustenance or protection. It was purposefully adapted into a hedging plant when the peasants were thrown off their 'inherited' land by landowners, following the General Enclosures Act of 1845. Thus the peasant's tree, the faerie hawthorn, was turned into an instrument of division and derision by political and money-minded barons, a barrier hedgerow to keep people off the land.

PHYSICAL USES

Hawthorn wood is hard-wearing, but it only provides enough wood for small things. Anciently it was used to make handles, particularly of personal things necessary for protection, like knives and daggers. No wood burns more readily than hawthorn, even when green, and it is known as the hottest firewood, better even than oak for oven-heating. Excellent charcoal is made from hawthorn.

In Scotland hawthorn bark was used to dye wool black and in most country places hawthorn leaves were used to make a refreshing tea. Hawthorn flowers can be added to syrups and can make a spirituous wine.

Having hawthorn in the fields was known to make cattle thrive; and if the birthing of a calf was premature, the afterbirth was hung upon a hawthorn tree so it could magically protect the young calf and give it quick growth. Hawthorn trees provide safe havens in thunderstorms, and along with the ash, apple and sometimes oak, it bears the mistletoe.

THE ASH TREE

IRISH/GAELIC	*Nuin*
OGHAM	
RUNIC	
RULING PLANET	Sun
ABILITIES	Inner and outer worlds linked. Marriage-bed of opposites. Quick intellect. Clarity. 'Aquarian Age' energy.
SEASON	Summer
ASH	*Fraxinus excelsior*. Deciduous.

The ash tree has toughness, strength and elasticity, and can grow up to 150 feet (45½ metres) high. It is a native of Britain and grows throughout Europe and America, being often found in ancient fossil beds. Its bark is ash-grey in colour and smooth to the touch when the tree is young, but it grows more irregularly ridged and cracked with age.

The strong leaves of the ash are compound, made up from four to eleven pairs of leaflets with toothed edges placed opposite each other on a central stalk, with a single leaf at the end. The leaflets have a conduit for water running down their centre stem, which is triangular in shape and is almost closed over. Hairs in this channel absorb moisture as it trickles down the mid-rib of the leaf. Water-absorbing structures are a feature of the ash tree.

After a leaf has fallen, a small horseshoe-shaped scar is left where the leaf stalk was joined to the twig. From this scar next year's black flower-buds will form.

There are no petals or sepals to ash flowers, only purple-headed stamens. After a few weeks the stamen-flowers shrivel and fall off to reveal the seed vessels; flat, lime green 'wings', hanging from long stalks. These seeds are often called 'keys', for in their winter state they were likened to bunches of medieval lock-keys. They have also been nicknamed 'spinners', for when they fall from the tree they spin in the air.

The roots of the ash spread out for some distance from the tree and tend to exhaust the soil. They sour the earth somewhat, which discourages other plant life from growing around or under the tree.

CUSTOM & LEGEND

The belief that the essence of humankind originated from the ash tree was extant in many ancient world cultures.

We are told that the ancient Greek goddess Nemesis carried an ash branch as a symbol of the divine instrument of the justice of the gods. Nemesis as daughter of Oceanus strongly emphasized the connections between ash and the life-sustaining qualities of water.

In northern European legend ash stands supreme as the World Tree, a symbol of universality which spreads its limbs over every land and forms a link between the gods, mankind and the dead. Odin hung himself on the Great World Tree to receive illumination in the form of the runes and so the tree became known as Askr Yggdrasill, Odin's magical steed. In hanging from the tree Odin made voluntary sacrifice in order to acquire hidden knowledge and wisdom. Gungnir, his great spear, was formed from ash and he used it to stir up warfare in the world, a state through which his followers could gain ecstatic frenzy.

The warriors of Odin were known as Berserks, i.e., 'bear shirts'. Berserk warriors took initiation by the mark of an ash spear consecrated to Odin.

The cult of Thor, less bloodthirsty than that of Odin, ruled the weather and sky and thus the crops. Thor was the epitome of the patriarchy, a god of the sky mythologically born from Mother Earth. His power was symbolized by his ashen spear and enormous hammer, and extended over the community.

The Vikings gained their title of *Aescling* (Men of Ash) because of their great reliance on the magic of the ash tree. Their magnificent vessels were ocean-going cargo carriers as well as war-ships, and while they were constructed of oak, all their magical parts were ash, for its sacredness to the battle-god gave great speed and control over water, along with an intoxicating physical prowess.

In Ireland the Viking culture rapidly established itself. To do so it used the magic of the ash tree, for in the early histories of Ireland it is said that three of the five magical trees which protected that land were ash, the other two being yew and oak. The fall of these trees was said to symbolize the triumph of Christianity over paganism, and is most probably linked to St Patrick who supposedly drove all serpents from Ireland with the aid of an ash stick in the fifth century AD.

HEALING

In early Britain the ash was associated with rebirth and new life, and was famous for its ability to heal children, who were passed through a split in the tree's trunk. The juice from an ash stick was customarily given to newborn children in order to protect them from harm.

The bitter bark of an ash branch was used to ease intermittent fevers. The bark from the root is even more potent, and in early medicine was used in treating arthritic rheumatism and liver diseases.

An infusion of ash leaves gathered when they exude their sticky substance in May or June, and powdered after drying, can be used to alleviate rheumatism. Ash is also used to give longevity and remove unwanted energies, spells and hexes, which in ancient times were thought to appear in the shape of warts.

MAGIC & INSPIRATION

Because of reverence given to the ash tree by the Teutons, after the Germanic tribes entered Britain *en masse*, ash replaced the birch as the species used for what would become called the maypole.

The druids carved magical images from ash roots, which they believed were every bit as powerful as mandrake. Their magical wands were also made from ash and were traditionally decorated in a sunwise-spiralling pattern. Ash wands make excellent healing wands because the tree is ruled by the health-giving sun and the best time for cutting them is at midsummer.

A cross of equal arms carved from ash wood can be used in sea rituals, for ash represents the great power of water. Such a cross was carried by sailors to protect them at sea or by land-folk for health and protection against malign influences. Ash was the traditional wood of the Yule log, burned to call back and celebrate the return of the sun-god at midwinter.

Many of the legends concerning ash refer to its speed over water and land, and its prolific use as spears and arrows testifies to its flight through air.

Ash is the tree of balance, the marriage-bed of opposites

which links our inner and outer worlds. Ruled by the sun, it contains the element of fire yet still responds to the subtlety of the more feminine water element. Ash reflects the Aquarian Age energy of quick clear intellect and strength of purpose, aided by keen intuition. Wands carved from ash are used for healing and solar magic, and all parts of the ash are used for protection, health and prosperity.

As a tree of ancient lunar associations which became symbolic of the might of the solar-gods, the ash is an interpreter and aligner of energies.

PHYSICAL USES

Ash wood is quick-growing, does not split when worked, and is the toughest and most elastic of all timbers. An ashen joint will bear more weight than any other kind. It was thus used in the construction of wagons, coaches, fencing-rails, oars, poles, furniture and implements.

On land, axles of ash enabled a carriage to move faster and handles of ash on working tools enabled a worker to do more.

Legend is full of witches riding through the air on ash

and birch broomsticks, and in later years ash was the second most important wood used in aeroplane construction.

Because of its elasticity ash was occasionally substituted for yew in bow-making. It was also used for the shafts of arrows.

In ancient Wales and Ireland the water-loving ash was used for coracle slats and oars. The Vikings used it to give special potency, speed and protection to their boats and weapons.

In later Britain ash became the Yule log, its burning seen as beneficial to the future prosperity of the family. Ash is the sweetest of the forest woods for burning, giving warmth to many ladies' chambers of the past.

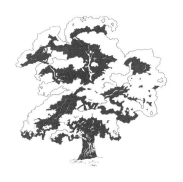

THE OAK TREE

IRISH/GAELIC	*Duir*
OGHAM	⌐|
RUNIC	〉
RULING PLANET	Jupiter
ABILITIES	Courage. Strength. Solid protection. Door to Mysteries. Health. Inner spiritual strength. To do with the element of Earth.
SEASONS	Summer; Autumn
ENGLISH OAK	*Quercus robur*. Deciduous.

The oak is a tree of great longevity and imposing stature, taking some 60 years to produce its first full crop of catkins, and gaining heights of 110 feet (33 metres) and girths of 30–40 feet (9–12 metres). There are over 400 species of oak in the world, ranging from trees to bushes, both evergreen and deciduous. The oak may live to well over 700 years, outliving all except the yew.

The English oak is known as the common or pedunculate oak, and is found in fields, hedgerows and woods. Along with the Sessile (or Durmast) oak (*Quercus petraea*), it is a native to Britain. The Sessile oak is most prolific in the forests of central France and the west of England. Its leaves are bigger and on a longer stalk than the English oak. The Holm oak (*Quercus ilex*) is common to the south of England and to Europe. 'Holm' is believed to be Anglo-Saxon for 'holly'. The tree adds to this association by its fondness of growing near holly, as well as by having holly-shaped leaves. The Turkey oak (*Quercus cerris*) is by far the most prolific of the species introduced to Britain.

Galls, produced by gall-wasps, grow from the life-giving sap of the trees. Known as oak apples, they look like hard brown balls at the ends of twigs. When insects lay eggs in the bark of the tree it goes on the defensive and produces such growths to protect itself.

In late April or early May the soft tender tufts of new oak leaves appear. Oaks are known for their production of 'Lammas shoots', which appear as we move into August and the heat of the summer. These new leafy shoots make the oaks glow with fresh colour at the time when all else seems to wilt from the heat of the sun.

The male catkins appear on the tree with the leaves in April. They become long, pollen-filled and pendulous by May. Then the female catkins open as upright flowers, which await the touch of fertilizing pollen from the males. They hold the seed vessels which will become acorns, the fruit of the oak tree.

By autumn the acorns have ripened. They have changed in colour from green to pale yellow to dark olive brown. Now the oak drops its fruit.

CUSTOM & LEGEND

The oak hosts many different forms of life. It is called a 'garden and a country', and because of its warmth and friendliness to man is regarded as an emblem of hospitality and strength. In the legends of many cultures acorns are said to have been man's first food. Traditionally, couples were married under oak trees long before the Christians substituted marriage in church.

The oak is possibly the most widely revered of all trees. The earliest spirits of Greek mythology were oak-tree spirits called dryads, and it was believed that oak was the first tree created by God from which sprang the entire human race.

According to Herodotus the sacred oak grove at Dodona had the greatest reputation for the gift of prophecy. Dodona was the oldest and most hallowed sanctuary in Greece and the goddess Dione (Diana) had an oak cult there until Zeus seized the oracle of Dodona and proclaimed it to be his. The oak grove of Dodona contained a far-spreading oak tree with evergreen leaves and sweet edible acorns. We are told that at the foot of the tree a spring of cold crystal water gushed and from its murmur inspired priestesses prophesied.

Jason's legendary ship, the *Argo*, was built from the trees of a sacred oak grove and the goddess Athene fitted an oracular beam into the ship's prow, cut from Zeus's oak at Dodona.

The Bible is full of references to oak. To the ancient Hebrews it was sacred and Abraham supposedly received his heavenly visitors under an oak. Jacob buried all the idols of Shechem under an oak, and under the Oak of

Ophra Gideon saw the angel who advised him how to free Israel. Saul and his sons are said to be buried under oaks, and when Augustine preached Christianity to the ancient Britons he stood under an oak tree.

Great oak forests once covered much of western Europe. The Celts with their thunder-god Taranis, the Germans, the Baltic tribes and the Slavs all worshipped within oak forests, forming holy groves in which to contact their awesome gods. In north-west Europe the oak was especially sacred to Thor, and Tacitus mentions groves held sacred to him at the end of the first century AD. Thunder-gods in particular are associated with oak, for as the tree's electrical resistance is low, it is struck by lightning far more than any other species.

The druids revered the oak above all other trees, because they believed it contained the energy, power and strength of their mighty god Esus. When it accepted the mistletoe upon it the oak became especially sacred, for the white berries of the mistletoe were seen to represent the sperm of the god.

There have been a great many famous oaks in British legend. The wizard Merlin worked his enchantments in a grove of oaks and supposedly used the topmost branch of an oak tree as his wand. King Arthur's Round Table was reputedly made from one slice of an enormous oak tree. The spirit of Herne the Hunter is believed to still inhabit an ancient oak tree. History tells us that Charles II hid in an oak following his defeat at the Battle of Worcester in 1651, and the tree was then named Royal Oak.

HEALING

The oak tree has a wide range of qualities suitable for healing purposes. These also aid the spirit and soul of the patient, especially when their vital forces have become strained and unbalanced. It is especially good as a tonic for adults and as a strengthener for growing children.

If ground into a fine powder, oak bark can be taken like snuff to stop nosebleeds. It can also be sprinkled onto sheets to alleviate the discomfort of bedsores. A strong decoction of oak bark is a good remedy for chronic diarrhoea.

Young oak leaf-buds were prepared in distilled water and taken inwardly to assuage inflammations. Bruised oak leaves are used outwardly, being applied to wounds and haemorrhoids to ease inflammations.

Oak bark, leaves and acorns make an astringent tonic due to their high tannin content.

The galls found on the ends of oak twigs are powerfully astringent, as though the essence of that quality of the tree has condensed within them in reacting to the insect which invaded it.

MAGIC & INSPIRATION

In druidic tradition the oak is used magically at all major celebrations, for through its legendary associations with the sky and thunder-gods and with the goddesses of fire and fertility, it is closely aligned to the solar cycle. Throughout the vital solar cycle the oak-gods are invoked for their aid at the quarterly celebrations of Solstices and Equinoxes. Oak-goddesses are invoked at the cross-quarters.

An acorn necklace can be made and worn during magical workings, meditations or celebrations as an aid in contacting the feminine energies of Diana and Blodeuwedd. Diviners often used oak galls to discover if a child had been bewitched. A healing 'oak-ball' was anciently made from oak bark or an oak gall. Once imbued with specific energies it was worn by those who needed healing.

Because the oak is so deep-rooted it can aid the well-being of our feet, the point with which we contact the earth. Many old oak recipes are for ointments which heal weary feet. Likewise an oak foot-bath made with a decoction of ground oak bark or leaves will not only soothe feet, but will also help them find the right pathway through life.

The druids were known as the 'wise men of oak', and the title 'druid' is most likely derived from *duir*, the old Irish/Gaelic name for oak. According to Nature mystics of all ages, the oak is a doorway, like all other trees. Through these doorways we enter other dimensions where we perceive different realities and worlds.

Throughout the centuries it has been said by woodmen and foresters that when an oak tree is felled it screams like a man. Oak spirits, or dryads, are usually depicted as wizened old men. They have a strong humorous presence which brings us a sense of release, showing that every problem is surmountable if we take nourishment from the earth.

An incredible example of an ancient oak grove is found on Dartmoor, unusual in that it is a miniature oak forest no more than 20 feet (6 metres) high. Wistman's Wood grows out of and between enormous lichen-covered rocks and boulders and is visually unique. A place once entered never forgotten.

Similarly magical are the two ancient oak trees called Gog and Magog that stand towards the back of Glastonbury Tor.

Side by side like husband and wife they represent the male and female energies of Nature which always guide the human race to fulfilment in life.

PHYSICAL USES

Because it is so hard and close-grained, oak wood lasts for centuries, and as it does not rot it was anciently used for bridges, piles for waterbreaks, and walkways over marshes.

The wooden walls of England's houses gave rise to the term 'hearts of oak', for the Englishman literally made oak his home. The oaks of the Forest of Dean became many a wooden wall and ship of England. As well as having incredible strength, oak wood is renowned for its beauty of grain and texture and its rich colour after polishing. Fighting clubs were made from oak wood, and roots of oak were used to make hafts for knives and daggers.

Oak trees of today are small compared to the earlier giants – a prehistoric boat of bog-oak was unearthed in Ireland, which had been dug out from one huge oak log, some 48½ feet (14½ metres) long.

As oak wood is impervious to alcohol it has always been used for casks in which to store liqueur. Many taverns and old pub-signs still express the ancient associations of oak trees.

Oak bark is often called 'tanner's bark' for it is used world-wide for tanning leather as the bark contains 15–20 per cent tannin. It is also used for dyeing.

Throughout many centuries oak leaves have been used to make good wines.

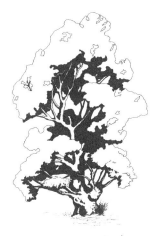

THE ENGLISH ELM

IRISH/GAELIC	*Lemh*
OGHAM	╞
RUNIC	ᚺ
RULING PLANET	Saturn
ABILITIES	Purification. Love. Light. Elves. Wisdom. To do with the element of Earth.
SEASONS	Summer; Autumn
ELM	*Ulmus campestris*. Deciduous.

The family *Ulmaceae* contains around 16 species of elm which are found throughout Europe and Asia. There are two kinds of elm in Britain: the English or common elm and the wych elm. Both are lofty and noble. The English elm is one of Britain's tallest trees, reaching heights of 150 feet (45½ metres) in a century of growth.

The shape of the elm tree is distinctly waisted and its branches fan out broadly into a magnificent canopy which acts as a massive receiver of light.

However, Dutch elm disease, brought into Britain from Holland in 1919, has claimed all the mature trees. Now when a tree reaches 30 years old it becomes vulnerable to the disease-carrying ambrosia beetle, which burrows into the bark and destroys the flow of life-giving sap. All mature elms are now gone. From noble trees living 400 years or more elms have become hedgerow trees doomed to die at 30.

All elm leaves are lop-sided at their base. The leaf-buds open in May to reveal leaves folded up like miniature fans, their beautiful pale green colour co-ordinating with the opened protective scales which are fawny-brown on the outside and pink on the inner. Elms are usually the first trees to flower in the spring. They flower and form their fruit well before their first leaves open.

In time the flower stamens shrivel and fall away to reveal bunches of flat green wings, each with a seed in the centre. These winged seeds quickly dry and turn light brown and paper-like. They are blown away on the wind almost at the time when the tree begins to open its leaves. Even though seeds are produced in vast amounts, they are rarely fertile, for the elm has evolved into reproducing via shoots and saplings which grow from the roots of old trees. While this method of reproduction has kept the elms' bloodline pure, it has not protected them in other ways.

CUSTOM & LEGEND

Ancient elms were part of the superstructure of the massive forests which once covered England. They dominated the landscape, standing proud and tall. Even as late as the seventeenth century, when the forests had all but disappeared, Culpeper stated elms were one of the 'most commonest English trees, overlooking Nature's seasons'.

In legend the elm has always been associated with death, the grave and theories of rebirth. In the Greek legend of Orpheus, when he returned to the upper world from Hades he began to play a love-song to his Lady

Eurydice, whereupon the first elm-grove sprang into existence.

Ancient Italian traditions encouraged a physical partnership between elms and vines. Elm trees were planted in vineyards to shade and protect the plants, and to give them a naturally branching structure to grow upon. This arrangement mixed the elm and vine legends, especially in themes referring to Bacchus, the Italian god of intoxication.

European legends concerning elms often refer to their associations with elves. If we look at the elven world we can touch the magical atmosphere that our ancestors associated with both them and the elm tree. In Britain elves were believed to give protection against lightning strikes and to help attract love. Such was their connection to elms that the trees gained the folk-name of 'elven' and such was their association with burial mounds that elms became incorporated into the death cycle, being literally made into coffins which housed the bodies of the dead.

The elm was integral to the farming calendar. The timing of its leafing was important as it showed farmers when the season was right to sow crops. The elm also forewarned, for when its leaves fell out of season it was taken as a sign that disease might come to cattle. This belief was particularly common in Devon, along with that which claimed that lightning would never strike an elm tree.

Elm trees once lined the hedgerows or grew in copses and all work of the farmers within the fields was influenced by them. Within the villages judges often dispensed justice from under the shade of elms.

Elms have always been a favourite tree for rooks, whose untidy nests and raucous shrieks would no doubt have boosted the dramatic imaginations of story-tellers, for birds were regarded as either containing the spirits of the dead or being totemic symbols of the mighty gods.

HEALING

Elm is a tree used to obtain purification. Physically it is used for cleansing the skin and making soaps, due to its astringent, anti-inflammatory qualities. Spiritually it is used for cleansing the spirit via meditation and use as an incense. Through this it also induces faith in yourself.

The inner bark was used to treat skin conditions and to alleviate rheumatism. Ulmin, a gummy substance which exudes from the bark in summer, was used as an astringent and for treating ringworm. A decoction made from the bark of the tree's roots, when fomented, was used to soften hard tumours.

The leaves or bark of elm, soaked in vinegar, clear scurf and it is recorded that they also treat leprosy. Bruised elm leaves were used to heal wounds, the leaves being packed around the wound and bound with elm bark. A decoction of elm leaves, when used like a warm poultice upon specific parts, is said to help broken bones mend.

The moisture found in blisters which sometimes appear on elm leaves (caused by a leaf-louse), if applied fresh, will 'cleanse the skin and make it fair', according to old recipes.

MAGIC & INSPIRATION

In magical work today meditation with elm aids the development of our communication with the devas, the spirits of the herbs, and by pricking an elm-leaf with a pin before placing it under the bed-pillow, divinatory dreams can be obtained.

Through its associations with funerary matters the elm was regarded as a tree that ultimately all would have to face – a tree of destiny. Yet to those who understood the ways of the natural world, death was regarded as a doorway to birth into another way of life, which is a far less sinister theory than that of Christian hell and damnation. Thus the elm tree, whilst being approached with respect, was also approached with reverence, hope and humbleness, for in the minds of the people any communication set up with the tree would be reflected in their passage from one life to another.

That the roots of elms are beneficial to the soil is agreed by folklore and botanists alike. The trees' health-giving qualities are reflected in the lush vegetation found growing around them; which houses many life-forms essential to the eco-system of the land.

The abundant canopies of ancient elms attracted light and the trees actually radiated, for while they drew light to them they also sent it out, encouraging the growth of living things.

So the death of ancient elms has robbed the earth of an integral part of its precious life-sustaining structure below ground and ecological balance above.

PHYSICAL USES

Elm wood is very tough and durable and does not split when worked, though it does have a reputation for warping. Because of this, the majority was used for rougher work in the construction of barns and houses. If seasoned well, however, it can be used for furniture. Cabinet-makers love it, for the rough bosses of its trunk form beautiful veins in the wood. It was also the wood used for coffins.

Elm wood is very durable in water, and as well as being used for shipbuilding, it was made into keels and bilge planks and used for water-pipes before cast iron.

Farmers in Britain encouraged elm in hedgerows and many elms were specifically planted as windbreaks. Cattle love eating elm leaves and in times of famine its leaves were collected as fodder for milk-producing cows. Dairy churns were made from elm to protect the milk from negative influences.

The inner lining of elm bark is very tough and fibrous and was traditionally made into ropes, string and mats.

THE BEECH TREE

IRISH/GAELIC	*Phagos*
OGHAM	᚛
RUNIC	ᛈᚺ
RULING PLANET	Saturn
ABILITIES	Old writings and knowledge. Rediscovering old wisdom. Wishes. Letting go of fixed ideas. To do with the elements of Air and Earth.
SEASONS	Spring/Summer; Autumn
BEECH	*Fagus sylvatica*. Deciduous.

Beech trees form deep shady woods, their thick leaves creating layer upon layer of canopy which screens out the light. They may grow 140 feet (42½ metres) high, with canopies up to 130 feet (40 metres) in diameter and trunks over 20 feet (6 metres) round.

Copper beech, with its beautifully coloured leaves, originates from Germany and has became a favourite garden or park tree in many parts of Europe.

In beeches the cambium layer is almost on the surface of the bark. This makes the tree very susceptible to injury, for all its life-giving functions are within this layer. It also makes beeches sensitive to light and trees which grow in the open branch low in order to give their trunks the necessary shade. When growing in woods beech trees shed their lower branches, as they then have no need to protect their trunks from light. Beech leaves are also sensitive to light and always twist on their stalks to face the sun.

By April the winter leaf-buds have swollen and opened to reveal folded fan-shaped leaves of a beautiful soft, pale but vibrant green. By summer the leaves are so abundant that often the stems and branches of the tree can hardly be seen. By autumn at the first touch of frost the beech wood becomes a place of immense colour, as the leaves turn from green to yellow, orange, russet and copper.

The beech tree's leaves open in April along with the male catkins. The female flowers appear by May and mature two or three days before the male flowers in readiness for the wind-borne pollen. Once fertilized, the female flowers develop into rough bristly brown husks containing two three-sided seeds which ripen by October.

Beech is not so long-lived as oak, but is linked to both oak and chestnut by having fruit formed in the same way, for the woody bract of the female flower grows to form a husk around the seed. Beech has a full crop of nuts every five years but does not really start producing a good crop until it is 50 years old. While beechnuts are nutritious for humans, eating too many can cause headaches or giddiness, as vast quantities of potash are contained within the tree.

CUSTOM & LEGEND

Beech, like blackthorn, is regarded as the 'Mother of the Woods', for it is protective and nurturing, giving shade with its canopy and food that can be eaten in its raw state. As a large tree of the broadleaf forest it is also known as the 'beech queen' who stands beside the 'oak king'.

In European legend the beech has a unique place, for it is especially associated with ancient wisdom and knowledge. On a material level we are told that thin slices of beech wood not only formed the first book (as distinct from scroll), but were also the first prepared surface upon which words were written. This would seem corroborated by etymology, for the Anglo-Saxon for 'beech' was *boc*, which became 'book'.

Books and scrolls are full of words, and in all ancient religions the god of learning or master of words was mighty. Whatever the word was written upon, be it wood, stone or hide, became imbued with the mightiness of the gods and the magic that they and their writing possessed. So beech received such reverence.

HEALING

Anciently it was stated that 'water found in hollow beech trees will cure both man and beast of any scurf or scab'. Coming closer to today, beech tar has been used as a medicinal antiseptic for eczema, psoriasis and chronic skin diseases. It is also an ingredient of an expectorant syrup used for bronchitis.

Beech leaves are cooling and binding. They can be applied to hot swellings as a poultice or an ointment. Dried leaves also aid patients when they are bedridden, for when put into mattresses or duvets they bring a therapeutic healing atmosphere to the sickroom, and a certain strength of Nature.

MAGIC & INSPIRATION

Because of its associations with the inception of writing, beech is linked to all written wisdom and we are aided in rediscovering the past through meditation with it. Indeed, when you feel drawn to beech, your subconscious is telling you to look to the past, for your answer to the present will be found there. Beech is the book of the past.

Magically, beech is specifically useful for making wishes. To do this, simply write or scratch your wish upon a small piece of beech wood, or a piece of bark or a small branch, and then in an appropriate spot, bury it. A small spell or simple words can be said during this process. As your written wish is claimed by the earth in which you buried it, so it will begin to manifest in life.

Carrying a small piece of beech wood is also a traditional charm used to bring good luck.

Legend tells us many stories of serpents and beech trees. The poet Tennyson also referred to the 'serpent-rooted' beech, and this distinction is most often seen when a beech tree grows upon a grassy knoll or bank, for then its surface-hugging roots are uncovered by the erosive action of the elements and are revealed as scrawling patterns of intertwined snake-like shapes.

In autumn days the shining green foliage of the beech wood is changed to gold, russet and brown, and, as some anonymous scribe observed, 'the low sun stares through dust of gold'. The fruit of the beech, now changed in colour to rusty gold, greatly enhances communication between people. Indeed, in times of stress, people once relied on eating beechnuts, not only to keep from starvation, but also as a collective action to strengthen communal or tribal ties. Nowadays, roasted beechnuts, prepared and eaten before a roaring fire with family and friends, evoke a warm glow of companionship.

Because of the smoothness of their trunks, beech trees evoke a strong tactile atmosphere. We want to approach and touch them, which makes them ideal for healing. This atmosphere is especially felt by lovers, as is witnessed by the many hearts, arrows and names that have been carved upon beech trees.

PHYSICAL USES

Beech wood is yellowish-pink in colour. It has a close, hard texture and is used for parquet flooring, chairs and small articles of treen. As it is close-grained it provides a beautiful surface to write upon. From my own experience it also takes paint well, for it is not as porous as other woods.

Because beech lasts well underwater, its long planks were ideal for shipbuilding in the past and in France peasant shoes (sabots) were traditionally made from beech wood to keep out the damp.

In Europe pigs are still turned out to eat acorns and beech-mast, and in France beech-mast is fed to pheasants and poultry. In England mast is used to feed park deer and also for fattening poultry, especially turkeys. In times of famine it has been used as human food, but it should never be fed to horses.

In America the nuts are made into beechnut butter, and the oil is used for cooking and lamp-lighting.

THE ROWAN TREE

IRISH/GAELIC	*Luis*
OGHAM	ᚂ
RUNIC	ᚲ
RULING PLANET	Sun
ABILITIES	Protection against enchantment. Protection of ley-lines. Protection of stone circles. Highest pure magic. Control of all senses. Healing. Psychic powers. Success. To do with the element of Fire.
SEASONS	Spring; Autumn
ROWAN	*Sorbus aucuparia*. Deciduous.

The rowan is a small tree growing up to 30 feet (9 metres) in height, with slender branches pointing upwards. Rowan branches rarely die and this enables the tree to keep its graceful shape for the term of its life, which can be upwards of 200 years. Rowan is a species of the rose family, along with apple, hawthorn and wild cherry.

The rowan does not form woods or forests on its own account, but rather joins in with other species of trees, aiding them by shading new saplings. As it needs plenty of light and air, it prefers high altitudes like the wilds of Scotland and is known to grow as high as 2,500 feet (760 metres) and more, hence the name 'Lady of the Mountain'.

In spring rowan's leaf-buds are covered in grey cottony down and are pressed close to the tree's twigs in a spiral. The toothed leaves are made up of many leaflets arranged upon a central stalk in six to eight opposite pairs, with a single leaflet at the end of the stalk. In this arrangement they are similar to the leaves of ash, which is why rowan is sometimes called the 'mountain ash'.

Rowan blossoms in May. Its creamy-white clusters of scented flowers weigh down the slender branches. Cross-fertilization of the flowers is aided by insects and once achieved the flowers fade, usually around the end of June.

As the season progresses, rowan berries ripen to a rich yellow-red. Rowan berries are a favourite food for birds, especially song-birds. They sing for hours after gorging themselves, and aid the propagation and distribution of the seeds during their flights.

By autumn, when the berries have mostly been eaten, rowan's leaves begin their colourful transformation. As the first frost touches them they turn from green to wonderful shades of gold, pink and scarlet, in which state they remain on the tree until late October winds strip the branches. The new leaf-buds are in evidence well before the old leaves fall.

CUSTOM & LEGEND

The rowan tree is small yet incredibly bold. Its leaves, blossoms and berries make exceptionally colourful statements on the face of the land. The legends associated with rowan are also bold and dramatic, making it a tree you cannot ignore.

The rowan is generally considered the feminine equivalent of the ash tree, and in Scandinavian myth the first woman was born from rowan and the first man from ash.

Rowan is also believed to have saved the life of the great god Thor by bending over a rapidly flowing river in which he was being swept to his death and helping him back to land.

In Icelandic myth rowan is particularly strong at the Winter Solstice, the beginning of the new solar year. At this time the tree is bare of foliage and when covered in frost appears as though covered in stars, powerfully expressing the outpouring light of the spirit in the darkest part of the year.

Yule legends say a special star glowed atop the mythical rowan tree, which heralded life returning to the world of darkness. The Christians later incorporated this star into their birth myths of Jesus and the star-clad rowan became a forerunner of our modern Christmas tree.

In Irish legend, the 'Quicken Tree of Dubhous' had marvellous berries which, if three were eaten, could transform a man of 100 years to 30 years of age! Another magical tree had the power, through its berries, to refresh people with 'the sustaining virtue of nine meals'. This tree was guarded by a particularly strong dragon.

Rowan is under the planetary influence of the sun and is strongly associated with two ancient sun-goddesses: Brigid of Ireland and Brigantia of England. Both these goddesses headed river and water cults and protected pastoral people and their flocks and herds. Brigid was renowned as a poetess, and in this visionary aspect was the Muse of the poetic and divinatory atmosphere which surrounds the rowan. These goddesses also possessed arrows made from rowan wood which could blaze with fire.

In Scotland the magical and protective qualities of rowan were recognized and utilized by Highlanders. The cross-beams of chimneys were often made from rowan and on Equinox and Solstice days rowan sticks were laid across the lintels to reinforce beneficial influences. In Devonshire and Worcestershire rowan was brought into the house on Holy Rood Day (3 May) to utilize its protective qualities.

HEALING

Warning: Rowan seeds are poisonous to children.

This said, rowan berries were prepared in decoction as a gargle for sore throats and inflamed tonsils. A strong astringent infusion was used externally to ease haemorrhoids and cure scurvy.

Rowan has been used since ancient times as an astringent and antibiotic. Through the visual senses it heals the human spirit. The calm atmosphere and beauty of rowan, the gracefulness of its spirit and the energy of life it represents, allow us to find healing, strength and purpose. To sustain such qualities, on leaving the tree select a small twig or leaf to carry away with you.

MAGIC & INSPIRATION

As a magical tree, rowan is used for all kinds of protection and vision. Incenses made from ground leaves and berries from the tree help us banish undesired energies. The druids of old used smoke from fires of rowan to call up spirit guides and magical spirits, and in similar fashion on a romantic level, people have always used rowan smoke to aid divinations of future loves and soul-mates.

Because rowan has white flowers it was deemed a tree of the goddess and as a visionary aid it invokes her when we need her help in choosing direction. Groves of rowan were preserved in ancient days as oracular shrines.

Rowan was a sacred tree to the druids and therefore predominates in the traditions of Western Europe. It is said that wherever druidic remains are found, so also is rowan. Magicians of old recorded spells on rowan staves and in the thoughts of the people magic became inherent to the rowan tree itself.

Irish legend is full of accounts of serpents and dragons guarding rowans, yet it goes unnoticed that the rowans themselves guard the earth dragons which express the life-force of the land. In Britain the ancient practice of placing stones upon powerful sacred spots has left us clues to the flow of the earth's energies, for a single stone was placed upon straight-flowing streams and circles were constructed upon coils or spirals. Spirals are the most commonly used symbol of the earth-dragon, for dragons were believed to coil themselves around hills. As a magical tree rowan guards the strong energy that the dragon represents.

The later Christians, in suppressing the old traditions, created saints to 'kill' such dragons as they claimed the traditional sacred places as their own.

At midsummer 'V'-shaped twigs of rowan were carried by travellers and it was advised that anyone travelling on Midsummer's Night should tuck a rowan sprig in his hat or horse's bridle lest he be transported to the land of faerie, for they are most active at this time.

Rowan gives protection when carried in any form, and if kept in the house protects it from storm and lightning. Its branches were used by Norsemen as rune-staves upon which to carve runes of protection.

PHYSICAL USES

Rowan wood is very tough. In the past it was used for ship masts and for poles and whips. Spindles and spinning-wheels were traditionally made from rowan wood cut between Beltaine and midsummer. Walking sticks can be made of rowan for protection while out at night.

Small branches of rowan were used to encircle milk and butter churns to protect the contents from thieves and evil, and goats were driven through hoops of rowan to ward off the 'evil-eye'. Rowan sticks were also used to divine the presence of metals underground. The bark and fruit of rowan can be used to dye wool black. The bark is also used for tanning.

Rowan was often known as the 'fowler's service tree', for its berries were used as a lure to catch birds. When times were hard in the land and corn was short, rowan berries (without their seed) were ground and used as a substitute for flour. They can also be used along with crab-apples in jellies and chutneys. Rowan jelly, which goes with lamb, pork and game dishes, can be made in late summer.

THE ALDER

IRISH/GAELIC	*Fearn*
OGHAM	ᚃ
RUNIC	ᚠ
RULING PLANET	Venus
ABILITIES	Divination. Oracular Heads. Protection of self and country. To do with the element of Water.
SEASONS	Spring; Autumn
ALDER	*Alnus glutinosa*. Deciduous.

The alder is native to Europe and Britain. It is found growing along the banks of streams and rivers or in low-lying
swampy land. It is a cousin of the birch and hazel and
often grows with them at the forest's edge, though, as its
seeds don't have 'wings' to become airborne, it needs the
water of a river or stream for their propagation.

The alder is a water-loving tree, and by bending its light
branches gracefully over a stream or river it creates shade
for plants and fish. It is usually a small tree but sometimes
reaches heights of 70 feet (21 metres). Four stages of production can be seen on the alder at any given time: the
old cones of last year's fruiting, the new leaf-buds or
leaves, and the male and female catkins of this year. Alder
is the only broadleaved tree to produce cones. It matures
at about 30 years of age and is then capable of a full crop
of seeds.

Alder can reach an age of 150 years. It is deceiving in its
appearance, for it is delicately proportioned yet has immense underlying strength. It is a beneficial tree both
above ground, with the shade it affords, and below
ground, where it enriches the soil by forming nitrogen
salts in its root system. Alder roots are many and tiny.
They draw moisture from the earth and love marshes and
swampy ground.

Alder leaves are held out horizontally. They are rounded and of an inverted heart-shape, with the broadest part furthest from the stem. When young they are somewhat sticky, for a gum is produced by the tree to ward off moisture.

Alder catkins form in the autumn preceding their flowering. They remain dormant on the tree throughout winter and open in the spring before the leaves. The female catkins have threads hanging from them which catch the pollen from the developed male catkins, after which they grow larger and become dark reddish-brown as the seeds develop within.

The ripe seeds fall in October and November. They have airtight cavities in their walls which allow them to float on water, along with a coating of oil to preserve them.

CUSTOM & LEGEND

As we look at the legends associated with the alder tree we can wonder at the might entwined within them, for physically the alder is a small tree. Its associations with the ancient beneficent gods gave foundation to the very magic of ancient Britain. But first, let us look at alder's world associations.

In ancient Greece Cronos was represented by an alder tree. In Italian tradition alder is also associated with the spring fire festivals and in Norse legends March was known as 'the lengthening month of the waking alder'. In Norse countries this specific time was called *Lenct*, and was a period of enforced fasting as the last of the winter's provisions ran low. When adopted by the Church and used for religious ideals, this time of fasting became Lent. In Irish legend the first human male was created from alder, and the first female from rowan. Alder was anciently regarded as a 'faerie tree' able to grant access to faerie realms.

Alder's associations with the element of fire are dramatic. In Ireland the felling of a sacred alder was said to result in the burning down of your home. Alder's burning qualities have always been prized amongst metal-workers and smiths. It was known for its hot charcoal, and used to forge ritual weapons.

As a tree which 'bleeds', alder is bound up in the legends of the Rollright Stones in Oxfordshire (*see also page 125*), where the King Stone, which stands alone and some way apart from the other stones, was once reputedly associated with a grove of alder trees. According to ancient legend, rituals were performed within this grove in which the sacred alders were cut to make them 'bleed profusely'.

When this happened, the King Stone apparently 'moved' in sympathy.

Alder was anciently renowned as the best wood to use for whistles and pipes, and this use gave it great affinity to the element of air. Such was the reputed harmony of the music played on alder pipes that the topmost branch of the alder tree became known as the 'oracular singing head' of the raven-god Bran, of whom so many tales were told.

The alder was regarded as the sacred totem tree of Bran and thus figures in many ancient legends of the West. The purple colour of alder's leaf-buds is especially associated with Bran, and is called 'royal purple'. In pagan Britain, such was the deep strength of feeling for Bran that the Christian Church had to acknowledge him, eventually sainting him into St Brons or Bran the Blessed.

HEALING

Alder has the ability to dissolve puffiness and the swellings of surface inflammation. Through its links with the element of water, it also has the capacity to heal our emotions. Its ruling planet Venus is reflected in the healing it can give, which particularly pertains to healing through the heart.

Culpeper recommended bathing in a decoction of alder bark to assuage burns and inflammations, and muslin soaked in the same decoction can be bound around the neck to ease inflammations of the throat.

Our forefathers, without doubt greater walkers than ourselves, used alder leaves to refresh their weary feet, putting them onto their bare soles.

Relief from rheumatism can be gained by loosely filling duvets or cushions with alder leaves, which can then be slept in or held on specifically painful areas for certain periods of time. The addition of aromatic herbs like lavender will enhance any healing.

MAGIC & INSPIRATION

Because of its ability to produce strongly coloured dyes, the alder tree is closely associated with the skills of dyers, spinners and weavers, wherein magical intent can be 'woven' into cloth and clothing. In Britain the goddess who ruled the spindle and loom was Brigid, her totem tree, the rowan, being used to make spindles and other such implements.

The appearance of alder's purple buds in earliest spring shows that the tree is powerful from Imbolc to the Spring

Equinox. At this time, as the strength of the sun is visibly growing, meditation with alder places our feet firmly upon the earth, whence we can discern the coming season of light and make wise preparation.

As the solar energy waxes into summer the fiery qualities of alder are used to propitiate the old gods, as did the smiths and weapon-makers of old, whose crafts were deemed the greatest elemental magic.

Because of its associations with water alder is also powerful in the west of the year, particularly from the Autumn Equinox to Samhain. Then it can be used along with other divinatory herbs in incenses and decorations.

The druids recognized alder as a sacred tree and with alder whistles 'enticed air elementals and whistled up the wind'. Witches were also said to use such whistles to conjure up the force of the north wind.

The old legends tell us that alder gives spiritual protection during disputes, so if you know you're heading for an unavoidable confrontation, carry a piece of alder with you.

Shelter, comfort and warmth are all reassuringly offered by the alder, and through these we can redefine our purpose and path through life. As guardian of the streams and rivers, the alder also watches over the life-giving waters that promote the health of the land. In this it guards the spark of wonder which is your birthright.

PHYSICAL USES

Alder is held as proof against the corruptive power of water, for its gummy leaves resist the rains and its timber resists decay when in water. Then alder wood becomes as hard and as strong as stone, and for this reason it has always been used to make boats, canal lockgates, bridges, platforms, jetties and piles of lasting quality. Out of water alder wood is soft and splits easily. It is of no use in the dry ground as posts and fences, for it decays rapidly.

Alder grown in England was used for making clogs, for it was soft, easy to work, warm and waterproof. Musical pipes, spinning-wheels and cart-wheels were also made from alder, and in Scotland it was used for chair-making and was termed the 'Scottish mahogany'.

Many beautiful dyes are obtained from the alder tree. Leaves of alder were used to tan leather and are preferable to the bark and young shoots, which contain too much tannin.

Warning: While alder aids man in many respects it is nevertheless bad for horses to eat, for it makes them ill and turns their tongues black.

THE WILLOW TREE

IRISH/GAELIC	*Saille*
OGHAM	ᚄ
RUNIC	ᛦ
RULING PLANET	Moon
ABILITIES	Dowsing. Psychism via water. Night visions. Lunar tides and magic. To do with the element of Water.
SEASONS	Spring; Autumn (Samhain)
WHITE WILLOW	*Salix alba*. Deciduous.

Willows are common to watersides all over Britain and Europe and there are many species in the family: white, crack, weeping, bay, purple, almond, grey and goat willow, to name but a few. The weeping willow, grown as an ornamental garden tree, is native to China and was introduced to Britain in the eighteenth century. The white willow is largest and can reach heights of 70–80 feet (21–4 metres) and girths of 20 feet (6 metres).

The majority of willow leaves are long and narrow, and the leaves of the white willow are of a greeny-grey colour on top, with an underside of ivory-white. Willows flower and leaf in May, sometimes together or sometimes flower before leaf, according to the weather. The male and female flowers are on separate trees and willows rely on insects and the wind for pollination. Willows flower in the form of catkins, of which the males are the prettiest. They begin as small silvery-grey silky buds that feel like velvet and from these buds grow long green catkins rather like caterpillars, with tiny scales which open to allow the stamens to appear. Willows allow their seeds to be scattered to the winds in fluffs of cottony-looking down.

The goat willow is more a bush than a tree. Its large catkin-buds are the true 'pussy willows'. After a few days the silky catkins develop into pyramidal sprays of yellow-headed stamens and this process, which takes the goat willow from a covering of silver to one of gold, is a very visual transformation. After all the pollen is distributed, the catkins begin to fall. Then the goat willow's leaves open. These are not of the usual willow shape, but are more a broad oval with crinkled edges, with a dark shiny topside and a downy underside.

CUSTOM & LEGEND

It is believed that Orpheus, regarded by the Greeks as the most celebrated of poets, received his gifts of eloquence and communication by carrying willow branches on his journeyings through the Underworld.

The Greek goddess Helice was associated with water magic and thus with willows. The priestesses of Helice were believed to use willow in every kind of water magic and witchcraft. In ancient times the willow-muse (or willow-tree faerie) was called Heliconian, after Helice. The willow-muse is sacred to poets, for the sound of the wind in willow trees influences inspiration.

The ancient Sumerian goddess Belili was a goddess of trees, and willows in particular. She also ruled over the moon, love and the Underworld. As a willow-goddess she presided over springs and wells.

Willow has many associations with funerary matters and has always been used as a funerary herb. Branches of willow were traditionally placed in coffins and young willow saplings were planted on graves. This is an echo of Celtic tradition, whereby the spirit of the corpse in the earth rises into the sapling planted above, which grows and retains the essence of the departed one. Burial mounds in Britain, especially when sited near marshes or lakes, were lined with planted willows in order to protect the spirits of the place. To 'wear the willow' once meant to grieve openly and garlands for mourning were traditionally woven from supple willow branches. The willow is still seen by some as an emblem of grief.

Pagan associations with willows have always been strong, for in the traditional sense they were revered as trees of the moon-goddess, she who reflects her moon magic upon the waters of Earth. In damp climates such as north-western Europe, willow was the tree most sought by the wise-women or healers, for it has great ability to ease rheumatism and other conditions aggravated by damp weather. Eventually the willow's medicinal and religious qualities fused and it gained the name 'witch's tree'.

Because of all these associations, the willow was regarded as a sacred tree and people have always been advised not to burn it lest grief befall them. It is thought that the origins of the saying 'Knock on wood' came from the age-old act of knocking on a willow tree to avert evil and bring good luck.

HEALING

Willow has always been used to protect against diseases caused by damp conditions. The bark and leaves contain salicylic acid, which is a good painkiller and the source of aspirin.

The Chinese see willow as a herb of immortality, for it has the ability to grow from the smallest branch stuck into the earth. It is thought that the priests of the Greek healer Asclepius used a particular variety of willow (*Angus castus*) to cure barrenness.

Gypsies make a bitter drink from willow bark for easing rheumatism, influenza and headaches. It is also a good tonic, but it is advised not to take more than three doses a day. Decoctions of willow bark can also be used to treat chronic diarrhoea.

Willow bark can be used as an incense to aid deep emotional healing, for it clears the head and uplifts the spirits.

When made into a strong decoction, the leaves and bark of willow can be rubbed into the scalp during hair-washing, before the final rinse, to eradicate dandruff.

MAGIC & INSPIRATION

As trees of enchantment, willows formed groves so magical that poets, artists, musicians, priests and priestesses sat within them to gain eloquence, prophecy and inspirational skills through meditation.

In pagan religions, willow is a tree of fertility. It is used at the Beltaine festival in either wand or bough form. Wands cut from willow, called 'willie-wains' in the north of Britain, are said to contain the power of water which is never truly still. The druids used magical wands cut from goat willow as protective charms. All parts of all willows guard against evil and can be carried or placed in the home for this purpose.

In traditional spells willow leaves are used to attract love. Wishes are granted by the willow tree if they are asked for in the correct manner. Willow leaves, wood and bark can be used in healing spells, especially as an ingredient of incense.

While willow is ruled by the moon, it is from its strong associations with Neptune that it gets its greatest visionary strength. Willows heal deep emotions and touch deep psychic levels within us, and because our deepest subconscious desires are difficult to face or deal with, especially primeval forces or 'raw' energy, it can be frightening to behold ourselves. That is why some have deemed willow to be 'under the power of the devil', though not, we may add, in pre-Christian times.

On female trees the silver catkins turn to grey spiky flowers, but on male trees they fill with pollen and turn to gold. Druids cut goat-willow wands from male trees, for the changeover from silver to gold was deemed very magical. The gold grains upon the silver were also regarded as a strong symbolic aid to the workings of the alchemists.

Many a legend tells of willow trees uprooting at night to stalk unwary travellers and such spooky tales have ensured that willow gets due respect. Willow is a tree of mysteries and of witcheries.

PHYSICAL USES

The wood of the white willow is light and tough. It was used extensively by builders for rafters and floors. The 'cricket bat willow' is a secondary species of white willow, and is used, as its name suggests, for the production of world-renowned cricket bats.

Willow is the native material for all kinds of woven basketry, for its supple branches are easy to weave and reliably strong. Willows were customarily pollarded in order to produce enough material for the cottage industries, the like of which in these modern days of plastic we can hardly realize.

Willow wood was used in the past in the construction of fast-sailing naval boats and for the bottoms of quarry carts which take a heavy, bumpy load. Willow was also used in the construction of coracles.

As already noted, willow's unique medicinal properties have always been recognized and used by healers. It is considered the natural form and source of modern aspirin and thus is often called the 'witch's aspirin'.

THE ELDER TREE

IRISH/GAELIC	*Ruis*
OGHAM	ᚏ
RUNIC	ᛗ
RULING PLANET	Venus
ABILITIES	Regeneration. Cauldron of Rebirth. To do with the element of Water.
SEASONS	Summer (early); Autumn (late)
ELDER	*Sambucus nigra*. Deciduous.

The elder seems to love to grow wild. It is found in abundance on wasteland, in chalk-pits, woods, hedgerows and gardens. It likes chalky soils, and while it is rare in Scotland, it is so common everywhere else that it is often ignored or considered a nuisance. It is anciently recorded that the trunks of elder trees grew to 6 feet (2 metres) in girth, though it is hard to visualize this when looking at our modern specimens. Today the elder is a shrub, bush or small tree which rarely exceeds 30 feet (9 metres) in height.

The elder has a peculiar method of growth. Several stems will appear at the base of a sapling, and each grows upright for a time and then droops over. The bud arising on the top of the curve created by the drooping stem will carry on growing upwards for a while, and then it droops over and growth continues from its upper-curve bud. By growing this way the elder trunk is not formed in one upward growing mass, as are oak and other trees, but is rather a patchwork of the curves of many drooping shoots, which is why the tree is never elegant nor of great height.

Elder leaves consist of five leaflets attached to a centre stalk and they are set opposite each other on the twig or branch. Because elder-buds are not protected by a weatherproof bud-case, the elder produces another, smaller bud in reserve beneath each main bud. Not long after the appearance of the elder's leaves its flower-buds form. By June they have opened and the tree is laden with their flat-topped masses made up of millions of tiny creamy-white flowers.

By autumn the berries ripen, turning into juice-filled, deep purply-black fruit, hanging in heavy bunches called drupes. Birds love elderberries and will swoop *en masse* to strip a tree. Having eaten the berries the birds void their seeds unharmed upon their flights, thus ensuring wide-spread propagation.

CUSTOM & LEGEND

The unique personality of the elder was anciently believed to come from the spirit of the 'Elder Mother' who dwelt within the tree. The Elder Mother worked strong earth magic and according to legend avenged all who harmed her host trees. No forester of old would touch elder, let alone cut it, before asking the Elder Mother's permission three times over and even then he was still in dread of her possible wrath. Likewise, in many country districts of Europe and Britain, wise people still show respect by touching their hats when passing elder trees, in continuance of ancient custom. Certain North American tribes also believe that elder is the Mother of the human race.

According to legend witches would often turn themselves into elder trees, and one famous witch-tree turned a king and his men to stone, thereby creating the Rollright Stones in Oxfordshire (*see also pages 109–10*). It is said that in ancient days on Midsummer's Eve people sought the elder witch-tree, dancing with elder garlands in their hair. At midnight the King Stone acknowledged the proceedings and turned his head to watch the dancing. The Rollright Stones are also associated with powerful healing and divinatory qualities. The King's Men form a circle and prayers for the sick were reckoned more effective if offered up in the centre of it. It was also believed that barren women would be made fertile if they went to these stones at midnight and pressed their bare breasts against them. On certain nights of the year the King's Men are still believed to change into human form, in order to go dancing down to a nearby spring to quench their huge thirsts.

The King's Men have always seemed impossible to count, almost as if the stones move as you walk round the circle. However there are known to be around 77 stones and according to custom, if anyone does get the same total three times, they will have great wishes fulfilled. According to folklore, if ever Britain is in dire need the entire Rollright army will awaken into human form.

Country folklore states that those who sleep under an elder tree will never awaken, for the fragrance of the flowers will transport them to the Underworld. In reality the white pith inside the branches of elder contains a mild sleep-inducing drug, so this is probably responsible rather than the smell of the flowers.

HEALING

Elder was used medicinally by the ancient Britons, Celts and Romans, for it was thought that the Elder Mother within the tree could cure 'all the ills of mankind'. Virtually every ailment of the body is cured by some part of the elder.

Elder bark is diuretic and as a strong purgative its use dates back beyond Hippocrates. Young shoots of elder, eaten after being boiled like asparagus, clear the lungs and head of phlegm. Warts slowly disappear when rubbed with a green elder stick which is then buried in the ground to rot. The juice of fresh elder leaves eases inflammations of the eyes, and if sniffed, clears a stuffy nose. Elder leaves are diuretic, expectorant and purgative, and care should be taken if they are used internally, for they are somewhat toxic and can cause nausea.

Elder flowers are sudorific, diuretic, febrifuge and anti-rheumatic. A volatile oil is distilled from elder flowers. This is valued for use in eye and skin lotions but is most often diluted to form elder flower water. Elder flowers add fragrance to wine and are reputedly good for the voice. Elder flower ointment was used to heal horses of wounds in wars. The curative properties of elderberries are similar to the flowers, but weaker.

Magic & Inspiration

Elder was used as the wood of the pyre in cremations, and was also placed in the ground and the coffin at burials. It was anciently believed that wherever elder grew or rested was a sacred place, free from being despoiled.

In Ireland elder was used for handles in witches' broomsticks, and wreaths of elder twigs were woven as crowns and worn by witches at Samhain, to enhance their communications with the Otherworld and increase their ability to see the departed.

The flowering time of elder gives it a powerful status in late spring and early summer. Legend says that if we breathe deep of the blossoms' provocative perfume at midnight on Midsummer's Night, elder will 'open the portals to the faerie realms', and allow us sight of the faerie king and queen in their colourful, fleeting procession.

Pungent elder blossoms were traditionally used at weddings to bring good luck to the married pair. It was anciently believed that if a person was tempted to commit adultery they could carry an elder leaf to help them overcome temptation. Elder blossoms were used to bring good fortune to an unborn child, and in order to ensure a protected birth for both child and mother, pregnant women traditionally kissed an elder tree.

All growth of the elder tree was once considered sacred, for, like the Earth Mother herself, elder has been here since the beginning. It is an integral part of our flora and country magic, and, as we have seen, because of the great healing and support it has always given people, it has long been called the queen of herbs.

PHYSICAL USES

The elder is ancient in human history. Its hard close-grained wood was once used for fishing rods, and pith from the branches was sliced and used for floats. It was also used for shoemakers' pegs, instruments for mathematicians, combs and adult toys. Hollow elder sticks were blown through to encourage the burning of fires, and provide great fun for children, as they are easily adapted into whistles, pop-guns and blow-pipes. As well as the berries, the bark, root and leaves of elder provide a full range of natural colours used to dye wool.

Elderberries can also be used in the making of soups, puddings, jellies, chutneys, drinks and wines. Elderberry wine, a tonic wine known as 'poor man's port', was once so popular that huge orchards of elder were maintained in Kent to obtain enough fruit for the population.

THE POPLAR TREES

IRISH/GAELIC	*Eadha*
OGHAM	≣
RUNIC	↓
RULING PLANETS	Mercury (aspen); Saturn (white and black poplars)
ABILITIES	(Poplars) Cycles of time. Incenses. To do with the element of Water. (Aspen) Eloquence. Psychic gifts from the winds. Aid to rebirth. Prevention of illness. To do with the element of Air.
SEASONS	Autumn; Winter
POPLAR	*Salicaceae*. Deciduous.

While poplars are abundant in Europe, Britain has four main species, and of these the aspen and white poplar are said to be native. The black poplar was introduced long ago and the spire-like Lombardy poplar was brought by Lord Rochford in 1758 from its true home in the Himalayas. The grey poplar is a cross between aspen and white poplar.

Poplars are lovers of moist lowlands and valleys through which rivers run. All species of the poplar family are alike in that they never produce male and female flowers on the same tree, and they all protect their leaves from excesses of moisture.

The rapid growth of poplars begins a few days from the seed settling into the ground. In their first season black and white poplars reach a foot (30 cm) in height and in 40 years will have topped 100 feet (30 metres). The growth of aspen is not so rapid and of all the poplars it remains the daintiest, as shown in the illustration.

Aspens are rarely still, for their leaves tremble at the slightest movement of air. In order that the tree's leaves do not stop pollination of its flowers by the wind, aspens flower before their leaves appear from brown sticky buds. Aspen leaves are heart-shaped and dainty. Their very long stalks are flattened in a direction at right angles to the blade of the leaf. This causes the incessant movement of the leaves. Aspen leaves are waterproof. At the bottom of each blade there are two minute cups lined with resin which catch and absorb moisture.

The white poplar is not a common tree. It is found mainly in southern Britain, where it attains good heights. It is a tall tree with a light grey trunk. Its green leaves have distinct silvery-white hairs underneath, which keep out the damp.

The black poplar is tall, with deeply furrowed almost black bark and branches which bend somewhat downwards. Its leaf-buds are pointed and very sticky, for they are heavily coated with a scented balsam which waterproofs the leaves. The leaves are green on both sides and are of a definitive ace of spades shape.

CUSTOM & LEGEND

Aspen, the smallest member of the poplar family, is also known as the 'trembling', 'shaking' or 'quivering tree', for its leaves and branches move continuously upon the slightest of breezes. Because of its rustling leaves it is also called the 'whispering tree'. In ancient days the wind was regarded as a messenger of the gods and anything closely attuned to it, like the aspen, was considered sacred.

Golden crowns of aspen leaves were found in burial mounds in Mesopotamia, dating from circa 3,000 BC. In legend crowns of poplar leaves were not only worn by heroes, but also allowed heroes to visit the Underworld and return. The tree is potently pagan, offering communication and entrance into the faerie realms for mortals. The traditional explanation of its trembling is that aspen has the acutest hearing of all trees, and that it moves continuously because of what it hears from afar.

According to legend white poplar gained its special leaf colouring from Hercules, for he made himself a crown from poplar leaves after killing the evil giant Cacus. Hercules then wore this crown into the Underworld, where the tops of the leaves were scorched with heat and the undersides were silvered by the hero's radiance.

The white poplar and the aspen are sacred to Persephone, the goddess of regeneration, who was reputed to have a grove of poplars in the land of the sunset in the West.

The black poplar is sacred to the death-goddess Hecate. In country tradition a lamb's tail was buried under every newly planted poplar tree at lamb-docking time, as a sacrifice to the goddess of death.

The black poplar almost 'weeps' with sticky balsam, a resinous oily substance, said to be the tears of the seven

Heliades, sisters of Phaeton. He was killed by Zeus, who was enraged when he borrowed the chariot of the sun from Helios and came so close to the earth that it almost caught fire. His sisters wept so bitterly that the gods found compassion for them, changing them into poplar trees and their tears to amber.

HEALING

Contact with an aspen tree gives us a special sense of endurance, which allows us to face harsh realities in life with the ability to endure and conquer. Anciently aspen was called a shield tree, not only for the fact that shields were made from it, but also because it shields a person on spiritual levels from the all-consuming darkness associated with fear. Meditation with the aspen allows us to focus on the light and move ever closer to it.

The trees also absorb our fears and this can be utilized during meditation or healing work. When our fears have dissipated, the trees then fill us with new vitalizing energy. You have simply to ask a tree for help, accepting fully that on its own levels it can see, hear, understand and perform, no matter how crazy that seems. The idea is to suspend your disbelief; not necessarily 'believing', but rather accepting that it is possible. For then it can become so.

An ointment made from black poplar-buds and their sticky balsam is good for treating bruises, inflammations and gout. White poplar was used to cure leprosy.

MAGIC & INSPIRATION

All the poplars possess three attributes: the ability to shield and resist; an association with speech and language; and an affinity with the wind.

The aspen is ruled by Mercury. Its special qualities are associated with the element of air upon which it never ceases moving. According to traditional recipes, poplar leaves and buds were added to 'flying ointments' which help induce the correct atmosphere for the practice of astral projection. Poplar leaves and buds were also used in money spells, for poplars were always believed to bring good luck in the monetary sense.

Aspen was used extensively by the Celts to make protective shields. On magical levels it protects against theft, shielding not only you but also your possessions from the attentions of others.

The planet Saturn is associated with large cycles of time and with poplar trees. The goddesses associated with poplars are also goddesses of the moon and powerful moon magic is associated with poplars. As this works within smaller time cycles (moons or months), it can be an excellent aid to our deeper understanding of larger time cycles (years and aeons).

Poplar trees have always captured the imaginations of artists, their tall graceful lines and ever-moving leaves enticing the senses to creativity. Renoir, Pissarro and Monet spent much of their lives in the poplar forests of France, capturing the mesmeric beauty of the trees upon canvas, using the portals to inspirational realms.

PHYSICAL USES

Poplar timber is of little value for it is a light wood. Aspen's wood, very soft and beautifully white, is ideal, however, for carving and sculpting. Crossing aspen with white poplar produced the grey poplar, which gives much stronger wood, which was used for a range of objects from silk rollers to sturdy barn-doors.

As white poplar wood does not splinter or catch fire easily, it was often used for floorboards in houses.

On water poplar wood is very buoyant, and for this reason it was made into oars and paddles. *Ebadh*, the Irish for 'aspen', translates as 'most buoyant of wood'.

In many European countries a poplar tree was planted at the birth of a daughter to provide a dowry for her when she came of age to marry.

As a symbol of hope the aspen was used by ancient Irish coffin-makers, being made into a *fe*, the measuring-rod used on corpses.

In times of scarcity cattle were fed on hand-gathered aspen leaves.

CONCLUSION

In ancient times Britain was known as a place of initiation and learning, where the qualities of the natural world not only sustained the people, but gave them a foundation upon which the structure of daily life was formed according to season. By acknowledging themselves as part of Nature they found inspiration, fulfilment and a sense of security, for they were attuned to the earth and its rhythms.

Today such a relationship is almost forgotten, for communication between people seems hard enough, let alone communing with Nature. We are all too busy in a world which has substituted roads for woodland and supermarkets for gardens.

The memories of trees are ancient. They show what was and what can be, giving us ecologically sound advice. The wild places where they grow and prosper, however, are now severely at risk, open to desecration in the so-called name of progress, their unique properties ignored as man and machine determine to control and alter the precious balance of the land. Yet we need trees to survive, for by holding the memories of what we were and the seed of what we will be, they form our identity as individuals and a race. Hence the conclusion to this book is dedicated to saving what remains of our trees and countryside, for as the land is covered in tarmac and concrete its essence dies, and so, little by little, do we.

As Wally Hope, the Stonehenge visionary (1946–75) says, 'The greatest evolution is by example.' It is by our waking up to understand that the earth comes first, for it is our home and provider of life. It is by accepting that we are but one species of a vast array of life-forms and that we do not rule. It is by acknowledging that we are utterly dependent upon the other forms that dwell beside us and the communication that we open up with them. Closest to us are the animals, then come the trees. They await communication and are willing to share their magic, for it is the key to our identity and the future of the earth.

Good Luck and Blessed Be.
Glastonbury 1995